THE ÆSTHETICS OF
WILLIAM HAZLITT

THE

ÆSTHETICS

OF

William Hazlitt

*A Study of the Philosophical
Basis of his Criticism*

By

ELISABETH
SCHNEIDER

1969

OCTAGON BOOKS

New York

Reprinted 1969

by special arrangement with the University of Pennsylvania Press

OCTAGON BOOKS

A DIVISION OF FARRAR, STRAUS & GIROUX, INC.

19 Union Square West

New York, N. Y. 10003

LIBRARY OF CONGRESS CATALOG CARD NUMBER: 71-86285

Printed in U.S.A. by
TAYLOR PUBLISHING COMPANY
DALLAS, TEXAS

PREFACE

THIS study has been undertaken in the belief that of all the prose writers of his time Hazlitt is the most modern, the least "dated," and that a more thorough understanding of his thought is therefore desirable. I have attempted here to supply a part of our deficiency in one direction, that of his philosophical and æsthetic thought. In a work of this sort it is perhaps impossible to maintain an entirely impartial attitude. I have not attempted, at any rate, to conceal my own liking for Hazlitt. On the other hand, not feeling—as many writers have felt—that even at this date Hazlitt requires defence, I have not, I hope, been inclined to misrepresent anything in his favor. But of this only the reader can judge.

Certain of my friends may catch glimpses of their philosophical ideas here and there, distorted generally almost beyond recognition. For those long talks during which my own ideas often became clarified, therefore, I wish to thank these friends, Miss Abbie Huston Evans and Miss Elizabeth McCord of Philadelphia, and Miss Kathleen Coburn of Toronto. I am very grateful also to my mother, who has indirectly done much to assist me. Most especially I am indebted to Professor Percy V. D. Shelly of the University of Pennsylvania, without whose generosity of thought and kindly advice this work would have been far more faulty than it is. I wish also to acknowledge the

v

many kindnesses of Professor Robert B. Wallace of Temple University.

The text of Hazlitt's works that I have used is that of the Waller and Glover edition. Mr. P. P. Howe's new *Centenary Edition,* although seventeen volumes have now appeared, is yet incomplete and has not reached the index volume, a convenience of the older edition which could hardly be dispensed with. In preparing this study for the press, however, I have made occasional use, as will be seen, of the material added by Mr. Howe in the notes to those volumes of his edition which have been published. I have also made extensive use, as all who write about Hazlitt must, of Mr. Howe's excellent biography of him.

E. W. S.

Rowe, Massachusetts
August 1, 1933

POSTSCRIPT, 1952

When the question of reprinting this volume first arose, I was tempted to embark upon revisions. These proved impracticable, though many pages glared at me when I reread them. Had I begun, I must have written a different book. After a lapse of years one is bound to see the same matter with an eye at least slightly changed. As any value this study may have lies in the matter and not the eye, I have let the whole stand except for the correction of some slips.

The late Mr. P. P. Howe's revision of the Waller and Glover edition was completed some years ago. My quotations from Hazlitt should be easily traceable in the new edition through the index volume.

E. W. S.

CONTENTS

INTRODUCTION

THE history of William Hazlitt's reputation has been a curious one. He has never, from his day to ours, lacked readers or admirers, but he has in a certain sense lacked recognition. The prose writers of the later nineteenth century read Hazlitt, occasionally borrowed from him—sometimes silently—but rarely said anything about him. Stevenson's eulogy of Hazlitt's essay "On Going a Journey" and his opinion that "though we are mighty fine fellows nowadays, we cannot write like Hazlitt" are exceptional, both in point of generosity and of whole-hearted enthusiasm. But even Stevenson, great as his admiration was—and, for that matter, considerable as his debt was, too—seems to have been interested chiefly in Hazlitt as a familiar essayist rather than in any other aspect of his genius.

Of late years, however, the attitude toward Hazlitt has changed somewhat, and the interest in him broadened and deepened. The admirable edition of his *Collected Works* by Waller and Glover, which appeared in the years 1902 to 1904, revealed to the public the breadth and scope of his writings and made possible a fuller appreciation of his many-sided excellence. A new and more complete edition of his works by Mr. P. P. Howe is at present under way, and an excellent biography, also by Mr. Howe, ap-

peared in 1922 and is now in its third edition. These publications are undoubtedly both signs and causes of an increased interest in Hazlitt's work. In addition to these
there have been several volumes of selections from
Hazlitt containing admirable introductory essays, such
as those by Professor Percy V. D. Shelly, Professor D.
Nichol Smith, and the more specialized *Hazlitt on English
Literature* by Professor Jacob Zeitlin.[1] Two other essays
of some importance have been written upon Hazlitt by
the late Professor W. P. Ker and by Professor H. W. Garrod.[2] And recently, in her *Second Common Reader* Virginia Woolf has published an essay upon him. But except
for one article, that by Professor Stanley P. Chase on "Hazlitt as a Critic of Art" [3]—limited for the most part to a
discussion of Hazlitt's criticism of Sir Joshua Reynolds's
theories of painting—and one short German dissertation
on Schlegel's influence upon Hazlitt's Shakespearean criticism [4]—except for these there has been no detailed or
extensive examination of any aspect of Hazlitt's work.[5]

The question may be raised whether any highly specialized studies of Hazlitt are either desirable or possible. So
much of the excellence of his writing has been assumed,
and rightly, to depend upon his intuitive perception of
what is best in literature and upon his insight into life and
his native zest for it, that there might appear to be noth-

---

[1] Percy V. D. Shelly, *Essays by William Hazlitt;* D. Nichol Smith, *Hazlitt:
Essays on Poetry;* Jacob Zeitlin, *Hazlitt on English Literature.*

[2] W. P. Ker, *Collected Essays,* Vol. I; H. W. Garrod, "The Place of Hazlitt
in English Criticism," in *The Profession of Poetry and other Lectures.*

[3] *P M L A,* Vol. 39 (1924), pp. 179–202.

[4] G. Schnöckelborg, *August Wilhelm Schlegel's Einfluss auf William
Hazlitt als Shakespeare-Kritiker.*

[5] Sir Edmund Gosse wrote an introduction, "Hazlitt as Art Critic," to an
edition of Hazlitt's *Conversations of Northcote.* But this contains little of
importance.

ing left for analysis. Yet to the thoughtful reader it is clear that in Hazlitt there converge certain lines of thought which do not appear as influences upon any other great English critic. He represents, for example, the influence of the earlier French romanticism in England in somewhat the same way as Coleridge does that of German romanticism. He was able, moreover, in a greater degree than any other English writer of his age to be a thorough-going romanticist, in certain respects at least, without having to belittle the achievements of English "classicism." These facts would of themselves lend historical interest to a somewhat more theoretical study of Hazlitt's criticism than has yet been made.

But there are more important reasons for such a study. However intuitive and personal may have been Hazlitt's criticism, it is difficult to suppose that a man who claimed to be first of all a metaphysician and only secondarily a critic [6] would have kept his philosophy and his criticism entirely distinct. That he did not consider that he was doing so is suggested by his assertion that he "hardly ever set about a paragraph or a criticism, but there was an undercurrent of thought, or some generic distinction on which the whole turned." [7] Nor was Hazlitt's claim to "metaphysical" powers of thought a figment of his imagination. Coleridge, whose standards in this respect were high enough, even when writing in a hostile spirit of Hazlitt said that his "vigor and originality" of mind and his "particular acuteness in speculative reasoning" would have

[6] His writings, he says, "are not, then, so properly the works of an author by profession, as the thoughts of a metaphysician expressed by a painter." —"On the Causes of Popular Opinion," *Collected Works of William Hazlitt*, XII, 319. (References to Hazlitt's writing hereafter, unless otherwise stated, will be to this edition under the abbreviated title of *Works*.)

[7] *Ibid.*, 319.

made Hazlitt the best of all persons to write a criticism of his (Coleridge's) *Lay Sermons*.[8]

Yet no attempt has been made to investigate this claim of Hazlitt's; it has, in fact, by implication been generally denied since his day. The theoretical side of his work has been either ignored entirely or traced to the influence of Coleridge. From the time of Alexander Ireland's account of Hazlitt as "critic and essayist" in 1889 [9] to the present day, attention has regularly been confined, on the critical side of his writing, to his treatment of individual writers and works. This is true of the essay by W. P. Ker,[10] of H. W. Garrod's lecture on *The Place of Hazlitt in English Criticism*, of Professor Nichol Smith's introductory essay,[11] and others. Saintsbury in his *History of Criticism* divides Hazlitt's critical work into two kinds. The first, in which Hazlitt "at least endeavours to be general," though "very stimulating, very interesting," Saintsbury considers the less valuable and less original of the two, for in this Coleridge is his "master,"·though Hazlitt succeeds in adorning his disquisitions with "more phrase" than did Coleridge.[12] Saintsbury leaves the matter at this and goes on to Hazlitt's criticism of authors and their works. With two exceptions, that of a very slight account of a few of Hazlitt's

[8] Coleridge, *Biographia Literaria*, ed. Shawcross, II, 214 (Chapter XXIV). —Hazlitt himself writes that when he was young and unknown Coleridge "used to say of me . . . that 'I had the most metaphysical head he ever met with.' "—*A Reply to Z.* —A none too discerning reviewer of Hazlitt's *Dramatic Literature of the Age of Elizabeth* in Gold's *London Magazine* for March, 1820 (I, 281 ff.) pays Hazlitt a somewhat similar tribute. Having advised him to avoid the low company of Lamb, Shelley, Coleridge, and Keats, as men very much his inferiors, the reviewer remarks that even Hazlitt is not much above the better class of essayists, "except in his metaphysics—where he certainly is a master."

[9] Alexander Ireland, *William Hazlitt*, pp. xlviii–liii.

[10] *Op. cit.*, pp. 242–257.

[11] *Op. cit.*, pp. xxxi–xxxii and elsewhere.

[12] III, 254–255.

general pronouncements on literature in the introduction
to Zeitlin's *Hazlitt on English Literature,* and that of the
scholarly but limited discussion by Professor Chase, already mentioned—with these two exceptions there has
been no attempt to discover what Hazlitt's beliefs actually
were with respect to the arts which he loved. It is not necessary to disagree with Saintsbury's opinion that the concrete side of Hazlitt's criticism is the best and most
valuable part of it; this indeed is true and not to be questioned. But no entirely just or final estimate of his criticism as a whole is possible on this basis—so long, that is,
as one large and important aspect of it is ignored through
a preference for the other. And even this more valuable
part of it, his concrete criticism, loses a good deal of its
significance by being considered altogether in isolation
from the rest of his thought or only in relation to his
politics.[13]

The large bulk of Hazlitt's writing, and the fact that
the statements of his philosophical, æsthetic, and critical
principles are to a considerable degree scattered through
it and cannot be sought in any one place, makes it no
simple afternoon's task to repair for oneself this neglect
of Hazlitt's general ideas. The purpose of the present study
is, therefore, in the first place, to fill the gap in our knowledge of Hazlitt by examining the theoretical side of his
criticism, by setting forth what he actually thought on the
questions most important or most commonly agitated in
the æsthetic and critical writing of his day. It is the opinion
of the present writer, after a careful consideration of Hazlitt's principles, that they do on the whole represent a
consistent point of view toward the arts; that they are not

[13] No one seems able to write of Hazlitt's criticism without discussing
his political prejudices.

only consistent in themselves, but that they bear a consistent relationship to his "metaphysics" on the one hand and to his criticism of painting and literature on the other; and that they must therefore be considered as an essential part of his work. His theories, whether in æsthetics or in philosophy proper, are not as a whole either new or original; but in certain important respects they are unique in the thought of the great English critics. More than this, there are some phases of his philosophy which, in spite of antiquated terminology, are surprisingly modern; and these are the aspects which have most strongly influenced his criticism. Finally, there are certain points in his philosophical criticism, particularly of literature, in which he is in advance of, or has anticipated, even his most brilliant contemporaries. This being the case, it is manifestly impossible to arrive at a true estimate of Hazlitt's criticism, however completely we may give ourselves up to its stimulating quality, without understanding its theoretical side.

As no attempt has hitherto been made to give an account of Hazlitt's philosophy, it has seemed wise here to summarize his philosophical ideas in themselves before entering upon what is properly the subject of the present investigation. This is the more necessary in view of the fact that the writer has found it impossible not to question the common assumption that Hazlitt's critical principles as a whole were derived from Coleridge. This assumption, as has already been suggested, is made by Saintsbury, who not only speaks of Coleridge as Hazlitt's "master," but who in his passing remarks on Hazlitt's philosophical criticism says that the best specimen of it is the lecture "On Poetry in General" and that "a good deal of this is directly Coleridgean." [14] Zeitlin puts it far more strongly: "His [Hazlitt's] criticism may be said to imply at every step the existence of Coleridge's, or to rise like an elegant superstructure on the solid foundation which the other had laid. Hazlitt communicated to the general public that love and appreciation of great literature which Coleridge inspired only in the few elect." [15] Mr. T. M. Raysor in *Coleridge's Shakespearean Criticism* refers to "Hazlitt's brilliant but reluctant and contemptuous discipleship" of Coleridge.[16] Such is the prevailing view of the relationship between the two critics. But it is one which may be accepted only with great modifications. This is an additional reason for setting forth at some length Hazlitt's philosophical views; for the gulf that separated Hazlitt from Coleridge in philosophy was a wide one, and it was precisely the same as that which in the most fundamental sense divided their critical principles.

Finally, an attempt has been made in outlining Hazlitt's theories to indicate their source, so far as this is possible. If he did not owe everything to Coleridge, at least Hazlitt owed some debts elsewhere. The attribution of ideas to particular sources, however, has in his case its dangers, in spite of the fact that he was rarely backward in acknowledging critical or intellectual obligations. For the period of his greatest reading and of the formulation of many, perhaps most, of his ideas preceded for the most part the years of his writing, and he does not therefore give us as much aid as he otherwise might have done by specific references to his reading. It is often impossible to trace his

[14] *History of Criticism*, III, 254–255.
[15] Zeitlin, *op. cit.*, p. xxxix–xl.
[16] I, lxi.

ideas with certainty to a specific writer, for he may too
easily have found the suggestion for them in a popularized
form in one of the periodicals, which he seems constantly
to have read; or it may have come to him through the
channels of conversation.[17]

There are certain difficulties in the way of tracing Hazlitt's thought, for the variety of his interests and the catholicity of his tastes join with the circumstance of his being
primarily a periodical writer or a journalist to render his
work fragmentary in character. There is, of course, continuity in *The Characters of Shakespeare's Plays* and in
the three courses of lectures which he delivered on literary
subjects. But many of his best and most important opinions are uttered in the course of a political or a familiar
essay. In such cases the audience addressed or the mood of
the writer or both must be taken into consideration before
the opinion expressed can be properly evaluated in relation to Hazlitt's thought as a whole. It is characteristic of
the familiar essayist, as it is of the lyric poet, that different
pieces represent different moods, and that the author is
not in any way bound to explain to his readers differences
which might seem to imply a contradiction between one
essay or poem and another. He assumes and is granted the
liberty of writing at one time what he would not perhaps
maintain at another. Sometimes a writer will do this out
of real inconsistency of character or opinion; but often
the inconsistency is apparent only, and is reconciled
through its relation to a fundamental viewpoint which he
may or may not choose to explain. Hazlitt himself complains of the accusation of inconsistency brought against

---

[17] For this reason as well as for some others which will be mentioned
later it has been thought desirable to append to this study a list of those
works on philosophy, æsthetics, and criticism which we can be certain
that Hazlitt actually read.

him because he has written first a fault-finding essay "On the Ignorance of the Learned," and then one "On Pedantry" and its charms and pleasures. Both have their truth, as he says; yet it is not in the nature of the familiar essay as Hazlitt understood it that all the aspects of a topic must be included and reconciled within the same work. The student of such a writer, under these circumstances, must do the best he can to see what threads of thought or feeling unite the divergent expressions; but in doing this he must guard against the temptation to reconcile apparent contradictions by his own connecting threads instead of those of his author.

I

Hazlitt's

PHILOSOPHY

Backgrounds

AN eminent jurist has said: "The enduring contributions of thinkers . . . are not systems but insights.
Indeed, systems are apt to be overrefined elaborations of
penetrating glimpses into truth." This is not the view of
the professed philosopher; indeed a full admission of the
truth of this remark would constitute something like a
philosophical suicide. In one sense, perhaps, Hazlitt was
spoiled for philosophy by a tacit recognition of this idea.
Certainly he showed a frequent dislike of system-makers.
Yet he set out upon the metaphysical road early. By the time
he was twenty he had for the "four or five years preceding"
been plunged in a "gulph of abstraction" by his self-imposed
course of philosophical reading and thought.[1] And although almost all his professedly philosophical writing belongs to his early period, he remarked, as late as four years
before his death, that the only pretension of which he was
tenacious was that of being a "metaphysician." [2] Yet he
constructed no complete system, nor even left anything like
the material for a system, as Coleridge did.

Hazlitt's philosophical writing was not confined to any
one period of his life, nor to formal and professedly philo-

[1] "My First Acquaintance with Poets," *Works*, XII, 267.
[2] "On Envy," *Plain Speaker, Works*, VII, 98.

sophical works. It is to be found scattered among his political writings, his familiar essays, and his criticism—from the *Reply to Malthus*, which was published in 1807, to the papers "On Prejudice" which appeared in *The Atlas* in 1830, the year of his death. The most ambitious attempts to formulate his philosophy, however, were made during his earlier years. In 1805 he published anonymously his first work, *An Essay on the Principles of Human Action: Being an Argument in favour of the Natural Disinterestedness of the Human Mind, To which are added Some Remarks on the Systems of Hartley and Helvetius.*[3] This was the work which had cost him years of labor, which contained his one "metaphysical discovery," and of which he said in *A Reply to Z:* "There is no work of mine which I should class as even third rate, except my Principles of Human Action."[4] In 1807 appeared his abridgment of Tucker's *The Light of Nature Pursued*, which, however, contained no original work by him except the Preface.[5] At about the same time he was planning a book on the *History of English Philosophy,* to be issued in "One Large Volume Quarto (Price, 1£. 10 s. to Subscribers)." The prospectus for this, written

[3] *Works*, VII, 385 ff.

[4] Written in reply to the attack upon Hazlitt by Wilson in the *Blackwood's Magazine* of August, 1818. The *Reply* was first published in full in 1923.

[5] The Preface has been reprinted in Hazlitt's *Works*, IV, 371 ff.—Hazlitt's philosophical reading sometimes turns up in his writing in odd ways. There is no doubt that Abraham Tucker is at the bottom of Hazlitt's well-known essay "Of Persons One would Wish to have Seen." In a section called "The Vision" (Bk. III, ch. XII), which Hazlitt particularly admired, occurs a passage in which Tucker tells of a supper with his friends. The company fell to considering how they would gratify their curiosity if they could charm up persons from the shades, and what questions they would ask. "One was for seeing his relations and friends again; another for a tête-à-tête with Elizabeth, or Mary Queen of Scots; others were for calling up Belisareus, Cicero, Archimedes, Alexander, and the heroes and sages of antiquity." Probably after reading this Hazlitt himself introduced the subject at Lamb's.

in 1808,[6] contains a comprehensive statement of his philosophical point of view. In 1812 Hazlitt delivered a series of ten lectures on English philosophy at the Russell Institution. Some considerable fragments of these were published by his son from manuscript in the *Literary Remains*.[7] After this date Hazlitt's philosophical opinions must be sought in his periodical writings. Often in a familiar essay a passing phrase or paragraph may give a clue to his thought or may even develop a philosophical point in an informal way. There are also, however, a few definitely philosophical essays which appeared in periodicals from time to time. Of these the most important are the series of four papers contributed to the *Morning Chronicle* in 1814 under the title of "Madame de Staël's Account of German Philosophy and Literature," which consisted largely of passages repeated from the *Principles of Human Action* and the lectures on philosophy; [8] two papers on "Mr. Locke a Great Plagiarist," one on the "Doctrine of Philosophical Necessity," and one or two others in the *Examiner* for 1815 and 1816; [9] an essay on "Reason and Imagination" in the *Plain Speaker;* [10] and finally, two dialogues on "Self-Love and Benevolence" which appeared in *The New Monthly Magazine* at the end of 1828.[11]

In any study of Hazlitt's work it is necessary to bear in mind his faithfulness to the ideas and associations of his youth. He himself at the age of forty-three said with a mixture of apology and pride that he had not changed

[6] Published by Howe in *New Writings*, second series, 11 ff.

[7] They are reprinted in Hazlitt's *Works*, XI, 25 ff. The paper which precedes them in this later edition, on "Abstract Ideas," probably formed part of the same series.—See notes to XI, 563.

[8] *Works*, XI, 162 ff.

[9] *Ibid.*, 258 ff., 277 ff., 284 ff.

[10] *Works*, VII, 44 ff.

[11] *Works*, XII, 95 ff.

his opinions since he was sixteen, a fact which Coleridge, who was afflicted with the opposite character, considered a fault.[12] This lifelong consistency in Hazlitt accounts in part for both the strength and the limitations of his philosophic outlook. Although he had embarked upon his course of "metaphysical" studies at as unripe an age as Coleridge had done, his orbit was a much narrower one and had not the advantage of being extended by study at a university. Bred in the household of a dissenting minister of an intellectual turn of mind, he became acquainted very early with the names and persons of certain theological and controversial writers. Price and Priestley were his father's friends; and at the age of thirteen the future philosophical journalist was writing, in the form of a letter to the *Shrewsbury Chronicle,* an indignant defense of Dr. Priestley against the treatment he had suffered at Birmingham on account of his opinions.[13] The elder Hazlitt had studied under Adam Smith at the University of Glasgow, and was by his son's account a great reader of religious controversial folios. Some of Hazlitt's own early reading seems to have been among these books of his father's, and to have included such works as Jonathan Edwards's *On the Freedom of the Will,* for which, characteristically, he retained an admiration to the end of his life. In philosophy proper Hazlitt's early horizon was circumscribed by the English sensationalist school and their French successors— Hobbes, Locke, Hartley, Helvétius, Condillac, D'Holbach —together with a few writers of contrary views, chiefly Rousseau, Berkeley, and Bishop Butler. From the first his sympathy was with these last three writers as against the others.

[12] Hazlitt, "On Consistency of Opinion," *Works,* XI, 509.
[13] William Hazlitt, *Literary Remains of the Late William Hazlitt,* xxiv-xxvii.

It has been claimed for Coleridge [14] that he was the first in England to see the importance of answering the sensationalist philosophy on the basis of its failure to bring together all the different interests of the human spirit, and therefore to deal with the whole philosophical problem. This is, no doubt, true insofar as Coleridge has a place, through his influence upon English thought, in the history of philosophy, and Hazlitt has not. But as early as 1798, when Coleridge and Hazlitt first met, Hazlitt (then aged twenty) had already laid the foundations of his philosophic study. During their first conversation together Hazlitt attempted to set forth to Coleridge the plan for his future *Essay on the Principles of Human Action,* which was inspired by this same purpose of freeing philosophy from the confined view of the materialists.

It is important, nevertheless, to realize how far his own thinking, in spite of an almost instinctive opposition to these philosophers, was conditioned by them.[15] During the years in which he was trying to write this first *Essay* he seems to have had little acquaintance with the ideas of Aristotle, of Plato and the neo-Platonists, of Spinoza and Leibniz, or the later German philosophers, and it is safe to say that he never became more than superficially familiar with them. "I tried to read some of the Dialogues in the translation of Plato, but, I confess, could make nothing of it." [16] In a footnote to this passage Hazlitt tells of having tried to learn in conversation from Thomas Taylor, the Platonist and translator, something of "Plato's doctrine of abstract ideas being the foundation of particular ones, which I suspect has more truth in it than we

14 Muirhead, *Coleridge as Philosopher,* pp. 26–30.

15 It is unquestionably true that in escaping from their limitations Coleridge very soon outdistanced Hazlitt.

16 "On Reading New Books," *Works,* XII, 164.

moderns are willing to admit." As this essay was published only three years before Hazlitt's death, it is clear that he never acquired any first-hand or any very precise knowledge of Plato. This left him weaker in the hands of his enemies than he perhaps realized, and was undoubtedly one reason for his never achieving a wholly organized or integrated philosophy.

The greatest difference between the approach of Coleridge and of Hazlitt to philosophy lies in the fact that the former's was fundamentally religious and the latter's was not. Since Hazlitt was never very explicit upon the subject of his religion, it is perhaps impossible to say with entire certainty what his views were. Crabb Robinson, writing in 1849 an account of his early acquaintance with Hazlitt, says that "he was one of the first students who left that college [the Unitarian New College at Hackney] an avowed infidel." [17] William Carew Hazlitt, his grandson, would obviously like to defend him from a charge, which had often been made, of irreligion. He quotes a remark of Hazlitt's friend, the painter Haydon: "I never heard any sceptic, but Hazlitt, discuss the matter [Christianity] with the gravity such a question demanded." Carew Hazlitt thinks his grandfather might have replied, "How do you know, sir, that I *am* a sceptic?" [18] But contemporary testimony receives some corroboration from Hazlitt's own writings. It is clear from these that he had respect for the Christian religion and great admiration for the character and teachings of Christ. He criticized philosophical sceptics for narrowness in refusing to admit the beauty and ethical value of the Bible.[19] But he also criticized the ex-

[17] Howe, *Life*, 52.
[18] W. C. Hazlitt, *Memoirs of William Hazlitt*, I, 210.
[19] *Conversations of Northcote, Works*, VI, 391–392.

planation offered by Dr. Chalmers of an implied conflict
between Christianity and the new ideas in Newton's
Principia. The doubts, once raised, are real ones, Hazlitt
says, and Dr. Chalmers's scheme only "shows how impossible it is to reconcile the faith delivered to the saints with
the subtleties and intricacies of metaphysics." [20] Hazlitt
thinks "one of the finest remarks that has been made in
modern times, is that of Lord Shaftesbury, that there is no
such thing as a perfect Theist, or an absolute Atheist";
and the utmost in belief that we can attain to, Hazlitt
himself says, is "a strong habitual belief in the excellence
of virtue, or the dispensations of Providence." [21] "The
most patient thinkers," he says elsewhere, "are those who
have the most doubts and the fewest violent prejudices." [22]
In general, Hazlitt's references to religion have a distinct
tinge of scepticism and at the same time are marked by
what is for him unusual reserve. He is emphatic in saying
that a sincere religious belief is desirable: strong though
his dislike was to Catholicism, he considered "an interest
in something (a wafer or a crucifix) better than an interest
in nothing." [23] But he nowhere gives any clear sign of
having such faith himself. Still more, he rarely gives any
sign of feeling the need of it. But the materialist school
was opposed and overthrown in England for the most part
by writers of a religious temper, whose deepest instincts
were offended by its implications. Their motive and points
of attack were therefore quite different from Hazlitt's.

---

20 "Pulpit Oratory," *Works,* XII, 279–280.
21 "On Cant and Hypocrisy," *Works,* XII, 333.
22 Preface to Abridgment of Tucker, *Works,* IV, 375.—Cf. also *Characteristics,* xxxv: "Death is the greatest evil; because it cuts off hope." *Works,*
II, 359.
23 *Conversations of Northcote, Works,* VI, 376–377.

His Opposition to Materialists
Theory of Abstraction

Before the beginning of the nineteenth century, the materialists had already begun to lose their dominant position among professed philosophers; but their opinions had become, what was far more dangerous from Hazlitt's point of view, a commonplace mode of thought among statesmen, politicians, and Scotch reviewers. His attacks upon them (and nearly all his philosophical writing took the form of criticism of this school) were undertaken, then, not as a defense of religion, nor were they an attempt to work through philosophy to a personal religious faith. They were begun, partly from the pure philosophical spirit of enquiry, partly from a desire to demolish conclusions drawn from this philosophy which were inimical to his own ethical idealism, and which he saw as weapons in the hands of political reaction; and partly also from the wish to rescue certain values in literature and the fine arts which seemed threatened by it.

In his early years he appears to have had some idea of working out a systematic philosophy, but a doubt of his power to do this was with him almost from the start. "If I should ever finish the plan which I have begun . . . ," he remarks in a note to his earliest published work, his "Remarks on the Systems of Hartley and Helvetius." [24] The recently discovered "Prospectus of a History of English Philosophy," written in 1808,[25] gives some idea of what this system might have been. It lists ten principles

[24] Published with his *Essay on the Principles of Human Action* in 1805. *Works*, VII, 469 n.
[25] *New Writings: Second Series*, 17 ff.

which Hazlitt proposes to establish in the course of the
work. These include an attempt to show that the mind
itself is not material; that the understanding (that which
perceives the relations of things) "is entirely distinct from
simple perception or sensation," and that ideas are "off-
spring of the understanding, not of the senses"; that the
power of abstraction is a consequence of the limitation of
man's mind; that "reason is a distinct source of knowledge . . . , over and above *experience*" (which does not
mean, however, that he supports the doctrine of innate
ideas); that "the principle of association does not account
for all our ideas, feelings, and actions"; that "there is a
principle of natural benevolence in the human mind";
that "the love of pleasure or happiness is not the only principle of action"; and finally three other points involving
the question of free will and the sense of power. Even this,
however, is an outline, not of a complete philosophical system, but of a fairly comprehensive refutation of the sensationalists; and the statement of these principles here goes
much further toward the doctrines of idealism than Hazlitt's actual beliefs, as worked out on these points when
treated separately, ever went. The fact was that he had accepted the limitations of the field of philosophy as assumed
by the school to which he was opposed, and had adopted
their psychological approach, which in any case was natural to him, and their empirical method. This meant that
he tended to limit the whole subject of philosophy or
"metaphysics" to two aspects, the Lockean investigation of
epistemology, and the question of *value,* with its relation
to the motives of human action. Hence, in general he left
almost untouched some deeper philosophical problems,
such questions as that of reality and of causation, and the
problem of "self" and "other," the duality of thought

and its object. His neglect of these was not altogether due, however, to the one-sidedness of his reading.[26] He was perfectly aware of them as problems, but, unwilling to accept a religious or mystical solution, he at first confessed himself balked by them, and eventually came to regard their solution as beyond the powers of the human mind.

On the subject of *reality* he admits, in criticizing Hartley's physiological explanation of the association of ideas, that his own views upon the subject are unsatisfactory, as all must be "without first ascertaining (if that were possible) the manner in which our ideas are produced, and the nature of consciousness, both of which I am utterly unable to comprehend." [27] "I never could make much," he admits again, "of the subject of real relations in nature. But in whatever way we determine with respect to them, whether they are absolutely true in nature, or are only the creatures of the mind, they cannot exist in nature after the same manner that they exist in the human mind." [28] This, in spite of great admiration for Berkeley,[29] is the nearest Hazlitt ever comes to an acceptance of Berkeleyan idealism. But though Hazlitt believes—he does not as a rule question the reality of the objective world—that we cannot know objective reality *as it is in itself,* he does not

[26] It is possible that Hazlitt's philosophical reading was more extensive than his published work indicates. The "Contents" of his projected history of English philosophy include accounts of the Cambridge Platonists, the "Scotch School," and others of which Hazlitt does not elsewhere show a first-hand knowledge. But it is likely that he intended to "get them up" later, and it is doubtful if he ever did so.

[27] "Remarks on the Systems of Hartley and Helvetius," *Works*, VII, 445. Whether this attitude on the part of Hazlitt be looked upon as a sign of characteristic intellectual honesty or of metaphysical incompetence will depend, no doubt, upon the Hazlittean or Coleridgean—the "Aristotelian" or "Platonic"—leanings of the reader.

[28] *Ibid.,* p. 455.

[29] See *Works*, VII, 434 n. and often elsewhere.

deny a certain correspondence between the real world and our idea of it. The difference lies in the fact that "the forms of things in nature are manifold; they only become one by being united in the same common principle of thought. The relations of the things themselves as they exist separately and by themselves must therefore be very different from their relations as perceived by the mind where they have an immediate communication with each other." [30] He thus accepts a dichotomy of *object* and *subject*, and in all the passages in which he tries to throw light upon the nature of either he assumes that the relation of the two is something which we cannot know.

Hazlitt's essentially critical mind never, at least in philosophical questions, justified a belief by its being a desirable one; and here again it is plain why he was no system-maker. The religious temper cannot endure uncertainty and constantly seeks a point of rest. But Hazlitt did not object to philosophical uncertainty. In this he was like Hume, to whom he owed a good deal in general outlook, though probably not in specific points. And Hazlitt was convinced that the passion for certainty is in itself often inimical to the passion for truth. "If persons who are sincere and free to inquire differ widely on any subject," he says, "it is because it is beyond their reach, and there is no satisfactory evidence one way or the other. *Supposing a thing to be doubtful, why should it not be left so?* [31] But men's passions and interests, when brought into play, are most tenacious on these points where their understandings afford them least light. Those doctrines are *established* which need propping up, as men place

[30] *Ibid.*, p. 455–456. It should be noted that Hazlitt does not here suppose things in the external world unrelated, but only related differently. What this difference consists in remains vague.

[31] Italics mine.

beams against falling houses. It does not require an act of parliament to persuade mathematicians to agree with Euclid, or painters to admire Raphael. . . . What admits of proof, men agree in, if they have no interest to the contrary; what they differ about in spite of all that can be said, is matter of taste or conjecture." [32]

This is one of the fundamental points in which he differed from Coleridge and perhaps from any Platonic idealist. The need or the impelling desire in man for identification with something beyond and greater than himself is assumed as ground for the reality of such union in much idealist philosophy. Hazlitt could grant that the power to conceive of God and the desire for union with Him was a proof of man's nobility and of his superiority over the beasts, without feeling called upon to take the next step and assert on this account the objective truth of man's conception. "If religion is supposed to be a mere fabrication of the human mind, the capacity to conceive it" makes a difference still between man and beast, he says. "Whatever the truth or falsehood of our speculations, the power to make them is peculiar to ourselves." [33] On the limits of belief he says: "We cannot set aside those prejudices which are founded on the limitation of our faculties or the constitution of society; only that we need not lay them down as abstract or demonstrable truths. It is there the bigotry and error begin. The language of taste and moderation is, *I prefer this, because it is best to me;* the language of dogmatism and intolerance is, *Because I prefer it, it is best in itself, and I will allow no one else to be of a different opinion.*" [34] Hazlitt therefore re-

[32] *Conversations of Northcote, Works,* VI, 432–433.
[33] "On Cant and Hypocrisy," *Works,* XII, 337.
[34] *Conversations of Northcote, Works,* VI, 456–457.

fuses to carry any speculative belief beyond the point to which his empirical method would lead him.

It is essential to keep this attitude of Hazlitt's in view and to realize its extreme variance from the thought of Coleridge. The distinction is important not only in the study of their philosophy but in that of their criticism also. Their fundamental viewpoints were almost antithetical. Hazlitt's willingness to remain in ignorance or uncertainty of ultimate reality sets him apart from nearly all the other romantics, whose philosophy as a whole has been criticized in recent times by Croce precisely on this ground. Croce accuses the romantics, that is, of "treating those emotions and ideas which appealed to their sympathies as pieces of eternal reality." [35] Or, as Shawcross expresses it in relation to Coleridge specifically, to such a mind as his, "the vividness of any conscious experience is the measure of its truth." [36]

Hazlitt's reason for rejecting the sensationalist philosophy was, then, in some fundamental particulars quite different from Coleridge's. His first important object of attack was the sensationalists' theory of knowledge. He took as his point of departure its extreme form in Locke's description of the human mind as a *tabula rasa*, upon the passive surface of which experience inscribes its own record. This, Hazlitt says, is not enough to account for the phenomenon of human thought and its relation to action. Nor does the addition of Hartley's theory of association complete the account; for this principle would make of the human mind nothing more than a "colony of mites justling each other in a stale cheese." He agrees that there

[35] This opinion of Croce is quoted from A. E. Powell's *The Romantic Theory of Poetry*, p. 18.
[36] In his introduction to Coleridge's *Biographia Literaria*, I, xv–xvi.

are no innate ideas in the mind, and that the sole material
of thought is furnished ultimately by the senses. But this
does not mean that the mind is a passive receptacle.[37] As
we have seen,[38] Hazlitt professed himself "utterly unable
to comprehend" the nature of consciousness and the manner in which our ideas are produced. So are we all, to be
sure: But he was convinced of the existence of some *active*
principle or power in the mind, which operates upon or
makes use of our sense impressions. This he calls understanding or reason, though there is at least one passage
in which he clearly identifies it instead with the imagination.[39] He did not believe that this power could be
explained as mere "matter in motion," nor even as motion itself.[40] "To assert that the operations of the mind·
and the operations of matter are in reality the same, so
that we should always regard the one as symbols or ex-
ponents of the other, is to assume the very point in dis-
pute"; indeed the mind has "laws, powers, and principles
of its own, and is not the mere puppet of matter." [41]

In one aspect the mind is conceived as a sort of passive
mirror. "The mind of man alone is relative to other
things, it represents not itself but many things existing

[37] Hazlitt does not always rise above the temptation of attacking a theory
deliberately on its most unregenerate side. The validity of the "unfortunate
simile" of the *tabula rasa* with its extreme implications, was not generally
held by the English empirical philosophers. (Cf. Hazlitt's controversial
attacks upon Malthus, which he directs against the first edition of the
Essay on Population, while admitting that Malthus had modified his views
considerably in the second edition.)
[38] P. 19, above.
[39] For this, see p. 99 ff., below.
[40] Cf. Coleridge's belief in the mind as endowed with "instincts and
offices of Reason," which are essential elements in all experience, forcing
it "to bring a unity into all our conceptions . . ."—Muirhead, *op. cit.,* p.
101, quoting from Coleridge's *Aids to Reflection.*
[41] "Mme. de Staël's Account of German Philosophy and Literature,"
Works, XI, 163–164; *Lectures on Philosophy. Ibid.,* pp. 27–28.

out of itself, it does not therefore represent the truth by
being sensible of one thing [this in reference to the associationists' view that we can think of 'only one thing or
have one idea at a time] but many things (for nature, its
object, is manifold) and though the things themselves as
they really exist cannot go out of themselves into other
things . . . there is no reason why the mind which is
merely representative should be confined to any one of
them more than to any other, and a perfect understanding should comprehend all as they are contained in nature, or *in all.*" [42] This perfect comprehension of all is of
course impossible to the finite mind, but it is and should
be man's constant endeavor to achieve.[43]

An underlying difficulty in Hazlitt's conception of the
mind and of knowledge becomes prominent in his treatment of the problem of abstraction. Nature, or the external world which is the object of cognition, is manifold;
the mind is one. What can be the nature of the relation
between the two? This is perhaps an insoluble philosophical problem. But neither Hazlitt nor the associationists
seemed able to state it in such a way as to permit the difficulty to be crystallized and segregated. The problem,
therefore, pervades their entire treatment of abstraction
without coming to the surface. Because of this Condillac
"proved" that there are no abstract ideas in the mind,
abstraction being merely a matter of words; [44] Horne

[42] "Remarks on the Systems of Hartley and Helvetius," *Works*, VII, 457.
[43] This view has an important bearing upon Hazlitt's view of the aims
of representational art. There is an apparent contradiction between it and
his explanation (pp. 19–20, above) of objective reality and man's idea of
it as that which is manifold brought into one subjectively. But Hazlitt is
obviously thinking of different functions of the mind in the two passages.
[44] Hazlitt cites this from the fifth chapter of *La Logique.*—"On Abstract
Ideas," *Works*, XI, 8.

Tooke still more ingeniously proved that abstraction is a mere trick of etymology brought about through the convenient use of the past participle.[45] Opposed to these was the common view that abstraction is the highest power of the human mind.[46] Hazlitt set himself to oppose both these extremes by a theory scarcely less ingenious than Horne Tooke's: so far from supposing that we have no abstract or general ideas, or that they are the very highest achievements of the human mind, Hazlitt said the fact is that we have nothing else. "All our notions from first to last, are strictly speaking, general and abstract, not absolute and particular; and to have a perfectly distinct idea of any one individual thing, or concrete existence, either as to the parts of which it is composed, or the differences belonging to it, or the circumstances connected with it, would imply an unlimited power of comprehension in the human mind, which is impossible. All particular things consist of, and lead to an infinite number of other things. Abstraction is a consequence of the limitation of the comprehensive faculty, and mixes itself more or less with every act of the mind of whatever kind." [47] From this and other statements very like it, it is evident that Hazlitt lumped together abstraction, generalization, lack of precision, lack of a power of detailed observation—and the inherent limitation of man's cognitive power as well.[48] "Abstraction

[45] Horne Tooke, *Diversions of Purley*, Vol. II. See also Hazlitt's criticism of this in *Works*, XI, 119 ff.

[46] This view is of the greatest importance in relation to eighteenth-century æsthetic theories and will be considered later.

[47] "On Abstract Ideas," *Works*, XI, 1–2.

[48] It is not only Hazlitt who does this. Generalization and abstraction are well mingled in the empiricists' discussions of the relation between specific *men* and general *man*, etc. And these are the discussions Hazlitt is considering.

is a trick to supply the defect of comprehension," he says; [49] but he fails to perceive that, even by the terms of his own definition, by the fact that abstraction does help to supply our defect, it is a means of advancing human knowledge beyond what would be possible without it, and beyond what would be possible if it meant no more than lack of precision or detailed observation. He recognized the value of this power of thought at other times, of course. Actually what he was doing here was to evade the question of whether abstract ideas such as *truth, right* and *wrong, justice,* have an objective reality apart from the human mind, whether they are merely useful symbols constructed for convenience out of human experience, or whether they are conceived by a higher faculty in communication with a higher and more valid reality than that of sense experience. It was a question upon which Hazlitt never entirely made up his mind. Both his religious agnosticism and his hostility to the theory of painting represented by Sir Joshua Reynolds led him to distrust "abstract ideas" as much as innate ones; on the other hand his interest in philosophical speculation forced his own thinking into abstraction, and he was not without occasional nostalgic leanings toward a Platonism which would involve admission of the higher validity of certain abstract ideas.[50] In some of Hazlitt's discussions of this problem, moreover, there is a confusion due to his assumption that to have an idea of a complex or manifold object (and all objects, as he says, are complex) is the same thing as to have a complex or manifold idea—assuming, that is, that there are as many acts of cognition and as many "ideas" involved in

[49] Preface to abridgment of Tucker's *Light of Nature, Works,* IV, 374.
[50] See his reference to Plato already cited on pp. 14–15, above, and especially his remarks upon beauty, pp. 67–68, below.

the perception of anything, as there are parts or aspects in the object perceived [51]—this in spite of his reiterated conviction that "the mind is *one.*" [52]

A recognition, though not a resolution, of this contradiction appears at one point, when he says that in proportion to the distinctness or individuality of any impression, the number of different "acts of the mind excited at the same time" increases; that is, "in proportion to the individuality of the image or idea, . . . the thought ceases to be individual, inasmuch as the simplicity of the attention is thus necessarily broken and divided into a number of different actions, which yet are all united in the same conscious feeling." [53] When he turns away from the heat of metaphysical controversy, however, he reasserts his usual commonsense view. "We must," he says, "improve our concrete experience of persons and things into the contemplation of general rules and principles, but without being grounded in individual facts and feelings, we shall end as we began, in ignorance." [54]

Kant

It is an unfortunate circumstance that Hazlitt did not know German, or was not induced to learn it, for there is no doubt that a knowledge of Kant would have done much

---

[51] The clearest and most convincing exposition of Hazlitt's theory of abstraction is found in the article on Mme. de Staël.—*Works*, XI, 173 ff. This is nearly identical with his exposition of the subject in the *Principles of Human Action* and the essay on "Abstract Ideas."

[52] "On Dr. Spurzheim's Theory," *Works*, VII, 139, and often elsewhere.

[53] "On Abstract Ideas," *Works*, XI, 20. The idea is here confused in expression, probably because Hazlitt himself had not revised the essay, which was not published during his lifetime, but by his son at a later date.

[54] "On Reason and Imagination," *Plain Speaker. Works*, VII, 46. The contrast between Coleridge and Hazlitt on this point is shown clearly by a passage in which Coleridge explains his habits of meditation to Gillman: "It is now as much my nature to evolve the fact from the law, as that of

to deepen as well as to clarify for him the problems concerned with knowledge and the constitution and faculties of the human mind. Hazlitt would certainly have accepted much of Kant, and would perhaps have been enabled to formulate his own philosophic position in a more comprehensive and explicit shape. Hence there is some interest in tracing Hazlitt's approach to the great philosopher of the age. In his earliest works all Hazlitt's references to Kant (few enough) are favorable, but they do not indicate any direct acquaintance with his writings. The first reference appears in the preface to his abridgment of Tucker's *Light of Nature*, written at some time between 1803 and the end of 1805.[55] In this he says, "The object of the German philosophy, or the system of Professor Kant, as far as I can understand it, is to explode this mechanical ignorance [that is, the theory of mind offered by the sensationalist school] . . . , and to admit our own immediate perceptions to be some evidence of what passes in the human mind. It takes for granted the common notions prevalent among mankind, and then endeavors to explain them; or to show their foundation in nature, and the universal relations of things. . . ." The reference ends with Hazlitt's favorite quotation of the Kantian idea that "the mind alone is formative." [56] He quotes the phrase again in the philosophical lectures of 1812,[57] as a summing up of his

a practical man to deduce the law from the fact."—Letter to J. Gillman, April 13, 1816. *Letters*, II, 658.—Coleridge might have added that it was his nature to deduce the horse from the wish for it. Hazlitt shows here, as often elsewhere, a strong sympathy with the spirit of Francis Bacon, to whom he pays frequent admiring tribute.

[55] The work was not published until 1807, but evidence from a letter of Lamb's shows it to have been in the hands of a publisher by January, 1806. —Howe, *Life*, p. 88.

[56] *Works*, IV, 378–379.

[57] "On Locke's Essay on the Human Understanding," *Works*, XI, 81. This

own insistence that human knowledge is not possible on the sensationalists' postulates alone, but requires an active non-material power to perceive the relations between individual sensations.

Within the next two years, however, Hazlitt unfortunately met with Willich's *Elements of the Critical Philosophy*, on the basis of which he completely reversed his previous attitude toward Kant in a review published in the *Morning Chronicle* for February 3, 1814, of Madame de Staël's *De L'Allemagne*.[58] Willich was not an accurate interpreter of Kant's philosophy; he greatly overemphasized its Platonic elements; and these were precisely what would tend to antagonize Hazlitt. So in this article Hazlitt enters into a criticism of Kant, the great stumbling-block in whose system, "if the translation is correct," Hazlitt says, is his "notions *a priori*." These "seem little better than the innate ideas of the schools, or the Platonic ideas of forms, which are to me the forms of *nothing*." [59] There is a further development of the criticism here, and Hazlitt's later references to the Critical Philosophy are of the same nature. He "totally dissents" from Coleridge's encomium on "the great German oracle Kant" and his followers, whose system appears to him "the most wilful and monstrous absurdity that ever was invented." It is "too mechanical," "dogmatic," full of "deliberate truisms." [60] Much of the violence of this later denunciation of Kant is in reality directed against Coleridge: the comments appear in a long and indignant arraignment of the latter in

formed one of the series of lectures on philosophy delivered at the Russell Institution at the beginning of 1812.

[58] "Madame de Staël's Account of German Philosophy and Literature," *Works*, XI, 162 ff.

[59] *Ibid.*, p. 168–169.

[60] "Coleridge's Literary Life," *Works*, X, 143–145. Published in 1817.

Hazlitt's article for the *Edinburgh Review* on the *Biographia Literaria*. He still thinks, however, that Kant's "maxim that 'the mind alone is formative,' is the only lever by which the modern philosophy can be overturned." [61]

Hostile as he was to the current materialism, Hazlitt was unable by his own efforts to free himself altogether from its bonds; this is shown most clearly in his tacit acceptance (with occasional excursions beyond the paling) of the limitation of the field of what he called metaphysics to what are now considered mainly psychological problems. Temperamentally too opposed to neo-Platonic doctrines to find help in that direction, Hazlitt instinctively sought his own way out in the very direction of the Kantian philosophy. It is a pity therefore that he was unable to make use of the clarification which a genuine knowledge of Kant would have meant to him.[62]

It is possible, however—even probable—that unless Hazlitt had become acquainted with the Kantian philosophy in his extreme youth he would not have accepted it later. For Leibnizian ideas, to which access was easy, were already widely current as an influence counteracting materialism. Yet it is very doubtful if Hazlitt ever took the trouble to read Leibniz; at least he appears to have derived little if anything from him. The explanation of this, which seems odd in the face of Hazlitt's keen interest in metaphysics, is perhaps that, believing a complete philosophical solution impossible, he pursued the subject not as a search for this solution but rather from a keen relish for the exercise of his own analytical faculties. What he sought in the study of metaphysics was possibly not a

---

[61] "Mr. Locke a great Plagiarist," *Works*, XI, 290. Published in 1816.

[62] It is interesting to speculate upon what might have been the later course of nineteenth-century English philosophy if at this date Kant had had a non-Platonic English interpreter such as Hazlitt might have been.

philosophic point of rest from uncertainties so much as the constant intellectual activity of coping with an enemy. Probably, on the whole, he was impelled by a mixture of motives; at any rate, a recognition of the latter one helps to explain some of his philosophical limitations.

Coleridge and Perception
Hartley—Motives of Action

In his treatment of perception, in his emphasis upon feeling, and in his conception of nature may be seen most conspicuously the links between Hazlitt's philosophy proper and his æsthetic views. In these points also his views most clearly indicate his position as an exponent of romanticism. And in regard to them the question of Hazlitt's debt to Coleridge becomes important.

Coleridge held that "perception is an art, dependent on the discipline of the senses and the development of organized bodies of knowledge." [63] This is precisely Hazlitt's view. But Coleridge goes on to consider perception from the standpoint of science, showing how the science of optics, the laws and properties of atmosphere, laws of vapor and density, and others, are all necessary in order that we may be sure that what we think we see is true. It is possible, but not likely, that Hazlitt's attention was directed to this view of perception from his early acquaintance with Coleridge.[64] With Coleridge the point is somewhat incidental. With Hazlitt, on the contrary, it is a

[63] Alice D. Snyder, Coleridge on Logic and Learning, pp. 88 and 116–117.

[64] The reverse is also possible here as in many points, though it is never susceptible of proof, since Hazlitt did not begin to write until a much later date than Coleridge. The general question of the relationship of ideas between the two will be considered later. (See p. 84 ff., below.) In regard to the present point, their view was the normal "commonsense" one requiring no specific source, though it was a point neglected by the current philosophy.

cardinal truth, which determines the bent of many of his
philosophical and æsthetic ideas; moreover his interest was
in quite different applications of it from those made by
Coleridge. The latter believed that, besides the necessary
training and knowledge already mentioned, we must have
"some scheme or general outline of the object, to which we
could determine to direct our attention." [65] This is very
"Platonic" indeed, for it would involve, essentially, knowing the thing before it is perceived. To some degree, however, it has its truth, especially for scientific method: most
scientists now admit that their experiments are conducted
upon tentative hypotheses, that imagination even here out-
runs knowledge and guides its advance. But Hazlitt was
not interested in science, and his recognition of the force
of this principle probably came through his study of art.
He could spend a week, he tells us, studying the lines of
an old woman's hand in a painting by Rembrandt. This
realization of how much more the painter sees in a given
object than does the ordinary man, and of how accuracy
and subtlety of perception increase with practice, led him
to see the superficiality of the mechanical application of
the associationist psychology, where the assumption was
that whatever we look at we really see or take in. In a
peculiarly modern way he went beyond the current psychology in showing that the degree and acuteness, and even
the number of our perceptions are determined, not by an
"outline" in the mind as Coleridge said, nor by a spatial
juxtaposition of particles in the brain corresponding to a
previous temporal juxtaposition of objects in the external
world, but by a receptiveness in the mind created by a
combination of our previous associations and our emotional need or feelings—that is, by our interest, to which

[65] Snyder, *op. cit.*, p. 116.

both our original bent and our present mood contribute. [66]
This view of Hazlitt's, if it owes a debt to anything outside
his painting studies, most likely derives something from
Rousseau's suggestions in *Emile* upon the use of "interest"
in the education of children and, of course, to the deep impression which Hartley's theory of association had made
upon him, in common with all thinkers, in spite of his
denial of it as an adequate theory of knowledge.

It is impossible to trace with entire certainty Hazlitt's
theories of knowledge, of perception, and of the relation
between thought and action or the causes of action. For
one thing, Hazlitt was not given to defining terms, and the
same word is likely to mean quite different things at different times. This is partly due, no doubt, to the necessarily
popular character of all except his earliest writing, but it
is much more owing to his conviction that nothing in life
is sufficiently simple and clear-cut to be bound within the

[66] Coleridge expresses a very similar idea. In fact the degree to which
both Coleridge and Hazlitt accepted the principle of association was practically the same, and their primary objection to it was identical: that association is dependent far more upon states of feeling than upon "juxtaposition," etc.—For Coleridge's statements see a letter to Southey of August 7,
1803 (*Letters*, I, 428), also Muirhead, *op. cit.*, p. 199.—In this case if there
is a debt on either side it must be Coleridge's to Hazlitt, for when their
first meeting took place in 1798 Hazlitt was already critical of associationism
and had planned his attack upon it along with the materialist philosophy.
—"My First Acquaintance with Poets," *Works*, XII, 274; and the *Essay on
Human Action as a whole.*—Precisely what Coleridge's views were at this
date is uncertain, though he seems not to have parted completely with
Hartley's views until 1801 or shortly before.—See, for the evidence on this,
Shawcross, Introduction to *Biographia Literaria*, I, xxix–xxx, and Muir-
head, *op. cit.*, pp. 45–46. For his continued admiration of Hartley in 1798
see Griggs, *Unpublished Letters of Samuel Taylor Coleridge*, I, 94. See also
the general discussion of Hazlitt's relation to Coleridge, p. 84 ff., below.—
It may be worth noting here that Professor Muirhead speaks of Coleridge's
"apparent entire ignorance of Butler" (p. 139); whereas Hazlitt in "My First
Acquaintance with Poets" says that Coleridge (this was in 1798) praised
Butler's *Sermons at the Rolls Chapel* but that he did not speak of the
Analogy (*Works*, XII, 266).

limits of a definition. He does on one occasion in his early "Remarks on the Systems of Hartley and Helvetius" attempt to define his use of the term consciousness, "where any particular stress is laid upon it," as the equivalent of *"conscientia,* the knowing or perceiving many things by a simple act.' [67] But his usual aversion to definition is best —and most amusingly—shown in an essay on "The New School of Reform," [68] in which both parties in the dialogue (one being himself) are put to all sorts of shifts to avoid the necessity of defining "reason." In general, Hazlitt makes no distinction between the human *mind* and the *soul. Understanding* is sometimes a faculty of the mind or soul, and sometimes it is the mind itself. *Reason* is often identified with *understanding,* but often too it is used in a narrower, unfavorable sense as representing the kind of petty logic associated with some eighteenth-century thought. It is never [69] the Reason of Coleridge's definition, disregarding facts because in a realm above them; it is sometimes that form of mechanical thinking or "choplogic" which draws false conclusions because of a lack of observation or "understanding" of the facts. Sometimes, finally, it represents the higher and more active exercise of the understanding.

But besides the question of definition, Hazlitt's philosophy is made difficult to trace at this point because he failed to treat separately the problems of perception, knowledge, and action. Thus he goes from *reason* or understanding as constitutive of knowledge to *reason* as motivating the will, without making clear whether it is the

[67] *Works,* VII, 437 n. Published in 1805.

[68] *Plain Speaker, Works,* VII, 187 ff.

[69] Except perhaps on one occasion, in the *Prospectus* for his history of philosophy.—See pp. 17–18, above.

same *reason* in both cases or not. His main contention in reference to this last, the relation between action, will, and reason, is one of his favorite subjects of argument, and perhaps his chief ground of objection to the materialist and utilitarian schools. Human action is not, as they assert, governed entirely by the reason working upon calculations of self-interest. Passion, imagination, memory, reason, are the essential faculties of the mind; [70] and all (except memory) are capable separately or in conjunction of being the cause of action. Passion often leads to action that is contrary to self-interest. If the mind can thus be swayed against its own interest by one motive, why, Hazlitt argues, may it not also be swayed by other and less selfish ones? This leads to his favorite argument upon the "natural disinterestedness of the human mind." He tells of a Scotch woman who could not bear to use her green peas even though she knew they would spoil. Here the passion for saving, Hazlitt says, has become detached from the actual thought of self-interest and has become an ideal end in itself.[71] In somewhat the same way—the mental faculty which makes it possible is the imagination—he would prove that truly unselfish action does exist, that "benevolence" is not all "self-love," as the current philosophy held.[72]

[70] Cf. a similar passage in the essay "On Will-making," *Table-Talk, Works*, VI, 117.

[71] "The Main Chance," *Works*, XII, 79–80.

[72] This is a part of Hazlitt's philosophy that was of great importance to himself because it furnished the chief support for his political and ethical idealism. But it has little to do with his æsthetic, and need only be briefly summarized here. One part of his argument he perhaps owed to the notes and preface of Bishop Butler's sermons. He says, at least ("Self-love and Benevolence," *Works*, XII, 96) that Bishop Butler has answered the argument for self-love "in the most satisfactory way"; in the *Reply to Z* (p. 27) Hazlitt says his own idea is like that of Butler "but not the same." Butler's argument is founded on a distinction between the self as the object, and

Rousseau and "Feeling"
Hazlitt's Pluralism

Undoubtedly the reading of Rousseau at an early age fortified, if it did not determine, the bent of Hazlitt's mind in its emphasis upon "feeling." "It is the fashion at present among the philosophical vulgar, to decry *feeling*, both the name and the thing," he remarks in an essay on "Common Sense." [73] And it was one of the most consistent purposes of Hazlitt's life to compel the world to a recognition of feeling as a central fact in human existence. There is a subtle but very important difference, however, between Rousseau's and Hazlitt's attitude toward emotion, a difference, in fact, which makes a sentimentalist of Rousseau and not of Hazlitt. For with Rousseau feeling is always treated as a *value* in itself, an ultimate good, to be encouraged, increased, and indulged. Hazlitt, it is true, sometimes writes in the same strain. In an essay on "Reason and Imagination" he sets up the value of feeling for its own sake in opposition to the utilitarians' emphasis upon

the self as the experiencer, of love. Rousseau makes a somewhat similar distinction, in the fourth book of *Emile*, between self-love and love of self (*amour de soi* and *amour-propre*). But Hazlitt made (as far as I have been able to determine) his own original and most ingenious, if hardly tenable contribution to the argument. It is founded on the idea of the non-existence of future time and the consequent apprehension of the future by the faculty of *imagination* alone. *Imagination* is the faculty by which we sympathize with others; *imagination* is the only faculty by which we can "sympathize" with our own future. Our self-love and our love of others are therefore emotions of the same *kind*, experienced by the same faculty. They do not differ in degree of reality, though they may differ in vividness. This is one of the main arguments in the *Principles of Human Action* and it is repeated by Hazlitt more than once in his later writings. It was his great "metaphysical discovery." The intelligence and dialectic skill with which the contention is worked out and defended are not apparent in such a brief summary as this.

[73] *Works*, XII, 378. This essay was published, and probably written, as late as 1829.

material progress. "A calculation of the mere ultimate advantages," he says here, "without regard to natural feelings and affections, may improve the external face and physical comforts of society, but will leave it heartless and worthless in itself." "We have been so used to count by millions of late, that we think the units that compose them nothing," he says again [74] in terms which have a somewhat modern ring. And, written at about the same time, "they [that is, things which affect the feelings] ought to excite all the emotion which they do excite," for although feeling and imagination may be "very inadequate tests of truth," yet "truth itself operates chiefly on the human mind through them." [75]

The difference in the attitudes of Hazlitt and Rousseau lies in the fact that with the latter this value of feeling for its own sake is the central conception; with Hazlitt the value of feeling arises from its truth, that is, from the actuality of its existence. His line of thought is this: The English and French systems of philosophy investigate only our manner of thinking or knowing; the utilitarians rest their theories upon the reason of man; the literature and criticism of the eighteenth century assume that man is governed by reason: but all these writings are false insofar as they fail to recognize that men's actions are governed by feeling and passion as well as, and even more than, by reason. It is not, for Hazlitt, that emotion is an abstract good in itself, as it is with Rousseau, but that emotion is an essential (not necessarily an undesirable, and if it were so, yet an immitigable) part of human nature, and no system of philosophy, no scheme of human betterment, no art or literature or criticism can be a true one if it ignores

[74] *Plain Speaker, Works,* VII, 50 and 53.
[75] "On Egotism," *Ibid.,* p. 161–162.

or even wishes away this element of feeling. The idea is clearly expressed in the form of a criticism of Godwin in the *Lectures on the English Comic Writers.* Godwin's system is there said to be wrong because it separates the "influence of reason or the understanding . . . from that of habit, sense, association, local and personal attachments, natural affection, etc."; but no scheme for the improvement of man can take reason as an exclusive guide "unless man were, or were capable of becoming, a purely intellectual being. Reason is no doubt one faculty of the human mind, and the chief gift of Providence to man; but it must itself be subject to and modified by other instincts and principles, because it is not the only one." [76] This is a truth which Hazlitt was never tired of reiterating. It is a view which places him at as great a distance from Rousseau as the realist is from the sentimentalist.[77]

But we have yet to consider that which gives an underlying unity to all the activities of Hazlitt's life—to his philosophy, his criticism, even his personal relations with other people. Philosophically it sets him as much apart from Rousseau as from Coleridge, and as far from Cole-

[76] *Works,* VIII, 132.

[77] There is an interesting appendage to this emphasis upon feeling, which would be significant if Hazlitt had ever developed the idea. There is a sense in which thought and feeling are identified in his mind. In a criticism of Madame Pasta's singing he says, "There is a natural eloquence about her singing *which we feel and therefore understand*" (*Works,* XI, 300. Italics mine). And again: "He who has much to think of must take many things to heart; *for thought and feeling are one*" (*Works,* VII, 206). This is the materialists' own maxim (see Morley, *Diderot and the Encyclopædists,* II, 137–138) *sentir est penser,* which Hazlitt elsewhere quotes from Helvétius with the comment, "I believe that this is true of the human mind, because the human mind is a thinking principle, it is natural to it to think, it cannot feel *without* thinking; but this maxim would not be at all true of such a human mind as is described by these philosophers, which would be equally incapable both of thought, and feeling as it exists in us" (*Works,* VII, 453). Cf. Coleridge's statement that "deep thinking is attainable only by a man of deep feeling" (Letters, I, 353).

ridge as from any of the English or French empiricists. It is founded on his view of the problem of duality—how to reconcile the eternally incomprehensible idea of *self* and *other*. For him the impossible is to be achieved not through assimilation of all *other* into the *self*, but through the projecting of *self* into all *other*.[78]

In Rousseau there was a perpetual craving to *take in:* he wished to draw all things to him that he might experience all within himself; and he seems to have felt that this was the ultimate value in life. The empiricists' idea was not in one sense very different, contrasting with Rousseau's chiefly in the more objective character of their values: both might be called, from a hostile point of view, acquisitive. Coleridge's views ran sometimes one way and sometimes another: at one moment his aim (and his preachment to others) is to learn, to take in and absorb more and more in a perpetual self-development, or evolvement or enlargement of the self; at another point his aim is double: man reaches out to nature, and nature enters into man, and thus there is union. Most often in Coleridge there is the aim toward a mystical transcending of the self by reaching out to God. This transcendental solution of the dualism is the only one that either succeeds or creates the illusion of success. The others remain admittedly efforts, with perhaps a limited, relative success in seeming to break down the barrier. But the mystic, in his own feeling at least, does remove the barrier completely at moments. To the unmystical, however, this solution appears both illusory and evasive: the mystic transcends his own self by identification with another but *self-created* one, and therefore does not transcend his individual self at all but is spared by his

---

[78] This is not to be confused with the much agitated modern psychological classification of "introvert" and "extrovert."

illusion from any efforts to identify himself with what is really *other*. He may be said to eat his cake and have it. By the same figure, the Rousseauist simply eats it; while Hazlitt is driven by a sort of suicidal impulse to become the cake.

Perhaps this account will appear to be no more than a fantastic description of the difference between subjectivist and objectivist points of view, and perhaps one should let it go at that and should say only that Hazlitt adopted the ethics of Christ without the religion, especially since this objectivism—or, better, this *projectivism*—is not introduced by Hazlitt into any philosophical system as a deliberate effort to resolve the essential dualism in life. No explicit statement of it appears in his philosophical writings proper: it is in his more popular works that we find such a remark as that there is nothing truly "great, but that which looks out of itself to others," [79] or that the power of the philosopher and the poet lies in "the power of looking beyond self." [80] Or in a theatrical criticism he will complain of the French "want of nature," and will explain that by "nature" it is meant "that the mind identifies itself with something so as to be no longer master of itself." [81] Or again, the office of the drama, he will say, is to hold the mirror up to nature, "to enable us to feel for others as for ourselves, or to embody a distinct interest out of ourselves by the force of imagination and passion." [82]

But to say that this idea does not form a part of Hazlitt's formal philosophy, is not to deny that it had a powerful

---

[79] "On the Spirit of Monarchy," *Works*, XII, 251.
[80] "On Knowledge of the World," *Ibid.*, p. 304.
[81] "Madame Pasta and Mademoiselle Mars," *Plain Speaker. Works*, VII, 328.
[82] "On Reason and Imagination," *Ibid.*, p. 55.

directing influence upon it. The primary purpose of his most labored achievement, the *Essay on the Principles of Human Action*, was to establish the philosophic or psychological possibility in man's mind of extending the bounds of feeling and of developing an interest in the welfare of others which would be of the same kind, if not necessarily as vivid, as the interest in one's own welfare.[83] To prove this he felt that it was necessary to overturn the whole of the materialist philosophy, which he accordingly proceeded to do. The influence of this view upon Hazlitt's criticism is suggested by the quotations above, and will presently appear further.

Given the desire to dissolve the barrier between the experiencing power and the thing experienced by an effort of projection instead of assimilation, we might expect to find an emphasis upon variety, complexity, and dissimilarity, upon the manifold aspects of external creation; and this we do find throughout Hazlitt's work. Even the mind itself is complicated, and any system which reduces all principles of action to one simple principle is therefore wrong.[84] "Truth is not one, but many; and an observation may be true in itself that contradicts another equally true, according to the point of view from which we contemplate the subject." [85] As to the relation between man and the universe, the more a man knows, the more he realizes that "he is nothing, a point, a speck in the universe, except as his mind reflects that universe, and as he enters into the infinite variety of truth, beauty, and power contained in it." [86] A strong religious conviction of a God

---

[83] See p. 35 n. 72, above.
[84] "The Love of Power or Action," *Works*, XI, 263, and often elsewhere.
[85] "Characteristic CCCCXXXI," *Works*, II, 416.
[86] "On Egotism," *Plain Speaker, Works*, VII, 164.—See also the passage quoted pp. 23–24, above.

or Power presiding over man and nature would bring this
manifold universe into a conceivable unity, but Hazlitt
had not this conviction, though he did occasionally tend
toward a kind of pantheism which partly unified external
phenomena by a feeling that there is "one undivided
spirit" pervading nature's works. For the expression of this
he usually goes to Wordsworth.[87] But as a rule, though
he sometimes shared the feeling, he considers the "craving
in the human mind after the Sensible and the One" as
"a natural infirmity, a disease, a false appetite in the
popular feeling, which must be gratified. Man is an individual animal with narrow faculties, but infinite desires,
which he is anxious to concentrate in some one object
within the grasp of his imagination." [88]

The born pluralist is a rare creature: in most men the
assimilative impulse is stronger than the projective, the
desire for resolution of the many into one more powerful
than desire for dissolution of the one into the many. Hazlitt seems to come as near to being a pluralist as is possible
to a normally constituted man. This is the key to the most
important of his general views upon art and literature. It
is also the key to his catholicity of taste.

[87] "On the Love of the Country," *Round Table. Works*, I, 17 ff.—Also
"The Doctrine of Philosophical Necessity," *Works*, XI, 277.

[88] "On the Spirit of Monarchy," *Works*, XII, 241.—Hazlitt's pluralism
finds much that is kindred in Bacon. Cf. the statement, which Hazlitt had
certainly read, that "the human understanding, from its peculiar nature,
easily supposes a greater degree of order and regularity in things than it
really finds. . . . Hence the fiction that all celestial bodies move in perfect
circles." Bacon, *Novum Organum*. I: 45.

II

Hazlitt's

ÆSTHETIC THEORY WITH SPECIAL REFERENCE TO PAINTING

Imitation of Nature—Reynolds, Diderot

H IS philosophical pluralism, then, establishes the foundation for Hazlitt's conception of the æsthetic experience. Art is a means by which we resolve, or attempt to resolve, or have the illusion of resolving, the separateness of the experiencing self and the external world in such a way that *the self becomes a part of the world.* Intrinsic value resides in the world primarily and in the self only insofar as it identifies itself with the world. Man becomes wise in proportion as he realizes that "he is nothing, a point, a speck in the universe, except as his mind reflects that universe, and as he enters into the infinite variety of truth, beauty, and power contained in it." [1] Recognition of this principle of Hazlitt's thought gives new life and value to his tireless iteration of the old formula that art must "imitate nature." No writer ever said this as many times as he did; and no writer ever meant more by it, for to none—not even to Wordsworth—was "nature" more important. In this fundamental attitude toward art Hazlitt's position is consistent and unwavering: he holds firmly, that is, to the necessity of *giving oneself to the experience*

---

[1] "On Egotism," *Works,* VII, 164. See also the passage quoted cn p. 23, above.

rather than of making experience serve or aggrandize the self. From the standpoint of ethics this belief would lead logically to quixotism. Although Hazlitt did not indeed carry it so far in his private life, its influence upon his political economy in this direction is clear and consistent. Hazlitt's æsthetic, then, is of a piece with the other main streams of his thought. But it partakes of their romantic character less in his throwing over of old theories than in the new interpretation which he gave to neo-classic commonplaces.

Eighteenth-century critics of art and literature, with the weight of Aristotelian tradition upon them, in general agreed that art should imitate nature. At the same time they looked upon the mind of man as superior to "nature" in almost any sense in which this latter term was used. Hence the tendency was to see the arts as relatively unimportant drawing-room accomplishments, necessary to the education of a fine gentleman, but a diversion from rather than a part of the essential activities of life. In theory, the only escape from this dilettante view of art would be through the abandonment of the notion of imitation itself or else through a reinterpretation of the term *nature*. Sir Joshua Reynolds, who was too serious an artist to accept the superficial view, escaped from the dilemma, as we shall see presently, by a modification of the meaning of both "imitation" and "nature" in his theory of the Ideal. No more than Reynolds was Hazlitt willing to consider art a mere relaxation or a hobby-horse for the polite world, like grottoes and Gothic wallpapers, or a "copy of verses." He accepted the doctrine of imitation completely, but he maintained the dignity of art through his conception of the greatness and all-inclusiveness of nature.

In the sense in which Hazlitt uses the term, nature is

identical with reality. It represents all that exists, whether within or without the mind of man, and all its aspects are worthy of imitation, though some may be "higher" than others. Nature is the inexhaustible unknown, to be understood and experienced as far as man is capable of doing so. That it is not merely external, not "outward shews" of things alone, is made clear again and again in his criticism. The greatness of Raphael and Titian consists, he believes, largely in their power to represent what is "internal" in thought and feeling; Shakespeare "imitates that within which passeth shew."

In one respect æsthetic pleasure resembles science, deriving, as both do, indeed, from the unknown or the imperfectly known. The difference is that "science depends on the discursive or *extensive*—art on the intuitive and *intensive* power of the mind. . . . The one is knowledge —the other power." [2] Art is "the microscope of the mind . . . and converts every object into a little universe in itself." Imitation interests "by exciting a more intense perception of truth, and calling out the powers of observation and comparison." For knowledge is pleasure as well as power: we may not know why the excitement of intellectual activity pleases, "but that it does so, is a general and acknowledged law of the human mind. We grow attached to the mathematics only from finding out their truth; and their utility consists (at present) in the contemplative pleasure they afford to the student." [3] This passage is interesting from the fact that it recognizes a kin-

[2] "Why the Arts Are not Progressive," from a passage in the *Morning Chronicle* article published in January, 1814, but not reprinted in *The Round Table. Works*, IX, 489–490. (Appendix I).—Is this perhaps the origin of De Quincey's distinction between the "literature of knowledge" and "the literature of power"? See comments on this point, p. 117 ff., below.

[3] "On Imitation," *Round Table, Works*, I, 74–76.

ship between "pure science" and the arts, based on their disinterestedness; it also recognizes implicitly the quality of disinterestedness as a constitutive element in æsthetic pleasure.

There is a tendency among critics to overlook, in their preoccupation with all that Hazlitt has to say of man and his works, and of the characters of individual men, his great love for "nature" in the other sense—in the sense of all that is not man or man-made. A recent writer of an article on Hazlitt speaks of his having "got up" the subject of natural scenery by a trip to Llangollen Vale in preparation for conversation with the Lake poets.[4] The remark is justifiable if one considers only the passage on which it is based. But from many other passages it is clear that Hazlitt's love of natural beauty neither began nor ended with his visit to Coleridge in 1798. His reverence for external nature is indeed very like that of Wordsworth, with, in general, a slightly stronger infusion of pantheistic thought and a fainter tinge of Christianity. The significance of the contemplation of nature as Hazlitt sees it is shown indirectly in many of his descriptive passages. "There is something in being near the sea," he says in one of these, "like the confines of eternity. It is a new element, a pure abstraction." And he continues in apostrophe: "What is there in common between thy life and ours, who gaze at thee? Blind, deaf and old, thou seest not, hearest not, understandest not; neither do we understand, who behold and listen to thee! Great as thou art, unconscious of thy greatness, unwieldy, enormous, preposterous twin-birth of matter, rest in thy dark, unfathomed cave of mystery, mocking human pride and weakness. Still is it given to the mind of man to wonder at thee, to confess its ignorance,

4 *Times Literary Supplement*, No. 1619 (Feb. 9, 1933), p. 88.

and to stand in awe of thy stupendous might and majesty, and of its own being, that can question thine!" [5] But it is not only the great in nature that demands reverence. The very least object is in its totality beyond the comprehension of even "the combined genius and powers of observation of all the great artists in the world."

So wide, then, is the realm which the artist may "imitate." To find and express any one truth in nature is the highest prerogative of a human being. "Nature has a thousand aspects," and one man may scarcely draw out more than one of them. Whoever does even this much is a man of genius. "One displays her force, another her refinement. . . . Each does that for which he is best fitted by his particular genius, that is to say, by some quality of mind in which the quality of the object sinks deepest, . . . is perceived to its utmost extent, and where again it forces its way out from the fulness with which it has taken possession of the mind of the student." [6] In a certain sense Hazlitt would not even have the artist be "creative"; for "all that we meet with in the masterpieces of taste and genius is to be found in the previous capacity of nature; and man, instead of adding to the store, or *creating* anything either as to matter or manner, can only draw out a feeble and imperfect transcript, bit by bit, and one appearance after another, according to the peculiar aptitude and affinity that subsists between his mind and some one part. The mind resembles a prism, which untwists the various rays of truth, and displays them by different modes and in several parcels." [7]

This "nature" or "truth," however, which the artist sees

[5] *Notes of a Journey Through France and Italy, Works,* IX, 90.
[6] "On Genius and Common Sense," *Table-Talk, Works,* VI, 47.
[7] "Originality," *Works,* IX, 425.

and expresses, is not merely the obvious visible features of an object which may be stupidly copied. We see nature not with our eyes alone, but with "our understandings and our hearts"; [8] for nature is "deep, obscure, and infinite." [9] Thus the Dutch and Flemish painters of minutely realistic scenes are not to be thought equal to Raphael, for they (except Rembrandt) represent things as their eye alone directs: they do not bring to bear upon their subject the insight, the sympathy, and the feeling or passion which render the work of the greatest artists truly expressive of the object imitated. Since the spirit, the hopes and aspirations of man are in Hazlitt's view a part of nature, perhaps even the most important part, the painter's power to make these visible to the eye is his highest gift.

There is an important passage in his essay on "The Indian Jugglers" in which Hazlitt considers the relation of the artist to nature in a somewhat different light. It represents a moment in which he deserts his usual pluralistic viewpoint in favor of one which resembles Wordsworth's so-called pantheism. The true artist, he says here, is concerned with the "ever-shifting forms of an eternal principle, that which is seen but for a moment, but dwells in the heart always, and is only seized as it passes by strong and secret sympathy." This art can be taught only by nature and genius; it is suggested by feeling. "In seeking for it without, we lose the harmonious clue to it within." In fact, the themes of great art are objects of sight only as these appeal to taste and imagination, "that is, as they appeal to the sense of beauty, of pleasure, and of power in the human breast, and are explained by that finer sense, and revealed in their inner structure to the eye in return."

8 "Thoughts on Taste," *Works*, XI, 461.
9 "On Genius and Common Sense," *Table-Talk, Works*, VI, 46.

"Objects, like words, have a meaning"; and the artist is
the interpreter of this meaning. It is not the eye alone, but
the eye guided by feeling, that distinguishes a cold from a
warm tone in a deep blue sky. The color of autumn leaves
"would be nothing without the feeling that accompanies
it; but it is that feeling that stamps them on the canvas,
faded, seared, blighted." Altogether, "the more ethereal,
evanescent, more refined and sublime part of art is the
seeing nature through the medium of sentiment and passion, as each object is a symbol of the affections and a link
in the chain of our endless being." The power of seeing
nature in this way is largely constitutive of each of those
different faculties known as genius, imagination, and taste:
this power is a sensibility "awake to every change and
every modification of its ever-varying impressions." [10]
Here, then, Hazlitt believes in the existence of a single
eternal principle, a chain of "endless being," of which we
become aware only as we are also aware of the infinite
gradations and subtle variations of our impressions. This
is a quite Coleridgean application of the principle of the
"reconciliation of opposites." [11] It is in relation, however,
to the writing, not of Coleridge, but of Reynolds, that
Hazlitt works out his view.

Sir Joshua Reynolds's *Discourses on Art* are the most important pronouncement in England from the eighteenth-
century standpoint, upon the representative arts. Partly for
this reason Hazlitt devoted a good deal of attention to

[10] "The Indian Jugglers," *Table-Talk, Works,* VI, 82–83.

[11] For this principle, see Alice D. Snyder, *Critical Principle of the Reconciliation of Opposites as employed by Coleridge.* Such a passage as this
would invalidate the contention that Hazlitt was an entirely consistent
pluralist, if that contention were held. But only the *prevailingly* pluralistic
character of Hazlitt's writing is, or can be, maintained, just as with
Coleridge the prevailingly Platonic character of the thought, though not
without its contradictory elements also, is granted.

them, partly also for more personal reasons. Hazlitt's elder
brother John, the miniaturist, was a pupil of Reynolds;
and Hazlitt in his youth spent some time at his brother's
in London trying himself to become a painter. He must
thus have come indirectly within the sphere of Reynolds's
influence. Hazlitt considered his own theory of art to be
strictly opposed to that of Reynolds, although it is true that
he sometimes quotes with approval individual sayings of
the great painter. Yet, when each writer has finished modifying and qualifying his own general principles, there turns
out to be less difference than Hazlitt supposed between
their theories, except on the two important subjects of the
ideal and the desirability of imitating the ancients.

Reynolds admitted the general axiom that art must imitate nature, for, he said, "Nature is, and must be the fountain which alone is inexhaustible; and from which all excellences must originally flow." [12] And in a later passage
he voices with some eloquence what is precisely Hazlitt's
attitude toward nature: "He who recurs to nature, at every
recurrence renews his strength. The rules of art he is never
likely to forget; they are few and simple; but nature is
refined, subtle, and infinitely various beyond the power
and retention of memory; it is necessary, therefore, to have
continual recourse to her. In this intercourse there is no
end of his improvement; the longer he lives, the nearer he
approaches to the true and perfect idea of art." [13] But this
passage occurs in one of the later discourses, and even in
these there are few like it.[14] His customary belief is that

[12] *Discourse* VI.

[13] *Discourse* XII.

[14] Reynolds modified his views on imitation, nature, and the ideal as
he grew older, and his changing opinions may be traced in the *Discourses,*
which represent his lectures before the students at the Royal Academy during a period of twenty-one years. A careful account of these changes, and
of Hazlitt's criticism of Reynolds's ideas, is given by Stanley P. Chase in the

"there are excellences in the art of painting beyond what is commonly called the imitation of nature." He cites the poets and orators of antiquity as authority for the idea that "all the arts receive their perfection from an ideal beauty, superior to what is to be found in individual nature." [15] The point to which this brings Reynolds is that the artist must imitate not simply nature, but "the general idea of nature," which is the basis of all that is fixed in art or taste. He comes then to a redefinition of nature which permits him to retain the Aristotelian maxim. "The terms beauty, or nature, which are general ideas, are but different modes of expressing the same thing, whether we apply these terms to statues, poetry, or pictures. Deformity is not nature, but an accidental deviation from her accustomed practice. This general idea therefore ought to be called Nature; and nothing else, correctly speaking, has a right to that name." [16] So we should not say that Rembrandt is imitating nature when he represents an individual object with its imperfections. It is the painter's duty to learn, by careful observation and comparison of all the minute errors in "particular nature," that which is the "will and intention of the Creator," as manifested in "the external form of living beings," and to present this and

article already referred to (p. 2, above) on "Hazlitt as a Critic of Art." Mr. Chase points out that Hazlitt's first criticisms of the *Discourses* are based almost wholly on the early lectures, and he concludes that Hazlitt probably had not yet read, or at least had not read with care, the later ones. This is quite possible. It is also possible that, as in the case of his criticism of Malthus and of Locke, Hazlitt concentrated his attack upon the parts which he most disliked, ignoring the rest even though he was familiar with it. It will not be possible here to deal with the successive stages of Reynolds's opinions, or his change of emphasis, as they for the most part are; nor is it necessary to do so for our purpose, since Hazlitt himself treated the *Discourses* as a single body of theory without regard to chronology.

[15] *Discourse* III.
[16] *Discourse* VII.

this only in his work.[17] No single model is adequate because the "general intention" of nature is never completely fulfilled in any one object of a class. Reynolds does not appear to wonder why the Creator should not have succeeded in producing a single individual in nature perfectly according to His will and intention; nor does it seem to him presumptuous to suppose that man by observing the errors can arrive at the true intention behind them. Later he tells us that "imitation is the means and not the end of art," [18] that "the Art which we profess has beauty for its object; this it is our business to discover and express; the beauty of which we are in quest is general and intellectual; it is an idea that subsists only in the mind; the sight never beheld it, nor has the hand expressed it." [19]

This is but a brief indication of Reynolds's views, but it is sufficient to mark the trend of his thought. Nature, in neo-classical opinion, is greatly inferior to Art. But Art imitates Nature. Nature, then, in the sense in which it is to be imitated, must signify, not the common, mean appearances of natural phenomena, but rather what we might wish these to be, or—identifying human desire with the will of the Creator—the otherwise unfulfilled intentions of God. This means that art must imitate the *ideal* world and not the *real*.

Hazlitt, though he sets out to oppose Reynolds, does not do so as firmly on this question of imitation as on two other points. For if we take Reynolds's least extreme statements, his admissions that nature is after all the inexhaustible fountain of art, "refined, subtle, and infinitely various," and compare them with Hazlitt's insistence that the painter

17 *Discourse* III.
18 *Discourse* X.
19 *Discourse* IX.

must not rest content with the surface of things but must penetrate to the "meaning" or the "feeling" beneath, we may suppose them both to be talking of much the same thing. The difference rests largely upon the fact that Reynolds, true to the habit of the earlier period, tends to regard the faculty by which the painter apprehends his subject as primarily intellectual, whereas Hazlitt looked upon it as primarily emotional. The painter must have sympathy, imagination, and passion in order to apprehend those aspects of truth most worthy to be imitated. Expression, for example, "can only be given by being felt." For this fact Hazlitt in an article on "Lucien Buonaparte's Collection," in which French art is under discussion,[20] offers a rather modern psychological explanation. We distinguish all objects, he believes, partly by "habitual knowledge"; and this is acute in proportion to the interest excited, that is, to "the intensity of the feeling or passion which is combined with the immediate impression on the senses. Expression is therefore only caught by sympathy." He further remarks that it is generally accepted that a painter cannot give an expression which is totally foreign to his character.[21] The idea that Hazlitt's "nature" has a great deal in common with Reynolds's "ideal" is further borne out by Hazlitt's passionate devotion to those most

20 *Works,* XI, 238–239.
21 Cf. Hazlitt's remarks upon the art of acting: "The study of individual models produces imitators and mannerists: the study of general principles produces pedants. It is feeling alone that makes up for the deficiencies of either mode of study. . . . In all cases where a strong impression of truth and nature is conveyed to the minds of others, it must have previously existed in an equal or greater degree in the mind producing it." The emotion or quality represented, he continues, may not have been apparent in the player's own life, for he may have had so many and such varied passions that they checked each other.—"On Novelty and Familiarity." *Plain Speaker, Works,* VII, 297–298. See also *Works,* IX, 111–112, and many other passages.

"ideal" painters, Raphael and Claude Lorraine, and by his comparative indifference to the Dutch and Flemish realistic painters. That under the term "fidelity to nature" he could put up with a very considerable departure from literal truth is apparent from his saying that in Raphael "one spirit, that of truth, pervades every part, brings down heaven to earth, mingles cardinals and popes with angels and apostles, and yet blends and harmonizes the whole by the true touches and intense feeling of what is beautiful and grand in nature." [22]

There is, however, a very great difference in the practical extent to which Hazlitt and Reynolds believed the purpose of art to be achieved by literal fidelity to concrete or "individual nature." Reynolds recommended the use of individual living models primarily for practice. In finished works, at least, the actual object must be corrected, he believed, by an idea in the mind, this idea being a permanent possession of the painter derived in part from close observation of various forms of nature, but mainly from the great painting and sculpture of the past, in which, he said, observation has already been generalized into ideal

[22] "Why the Arts are not Progressive." *Works*, I, 162.—Cf. also his statement that Shakespeare imitates "that within which passeth shew . . . the thoughts of the heart," etc. (*Works*, I, 233).—Professor Chase in his discussion of Hazlitt's relation to Reynolds ignores most of the passages I have cited from Hazlitt on *imitation* and is inclined to accept as most characteristic Hazlitt's most heated remonstrances against Reynolds's notion of the *ideal*. His conclusion is that Hazlitt in theory held the most narrow and literal view of imitation (and it is true, many passages suggest this), but that in his concrete criticism he was more "romantic" and less literal. But Hazlitt's most reasoned theory of imitation was not that. His essay "On the Imitation of Nature" from *The Champion*, December, 1814 (reprinted in *Works*, XI, 216 ff.) opens with this statement: "The Imitation of nature is the great object of art. . . . It is certain that the mechanical imitation of individual objects, or the parts of individual objects, does not always produce beauty or grandeur; or, generally speaking, that *the whole of art does not consist in copying nature."* The distinction between a *copy* and an *imitation* was a common one in criticism of the period.

forms that are ready-made for us. Hazlitt, on the other hand, insisted upon fidelity to the individual object or model. All that is necessary to the painter, beyond the technical elements of his craft, is the ability to select his models, and the power *to see what is in them.* He need not invent, he need only understand by sympathy. The pre-eminence of the great masters "has constantly depended, not on the creation of a fantastic, abstract excellence, existing nowhere but in their own minds, but in their selecting and embodying some one view of nature, which came immediately under their habitual observation, and which their particular genius led them to study and imitate with success." The Dutch, he thinks, abuse imitation by not being selective. "We forgive them." For their pictures do at least show that there is nothing in nature, "however mean or trivial, that has not its beauty and some interest belonging to it, if truly represented." [23] In the Elgin Marbles, at the other extreme of grandeur, he considers it evident that "the chief excellence of the figures depends on their having been copied from nature, and not from imagination." [24]

On this question of the fidelity of the painter to an individual model, as well as on the wider one of nature's "incorrectness," as Sir Joshua and the neo-classicists would have it, Hazlitt is perhaps indebted to Diderot, to whose ideas his own bear a close resemblance at many points. The resemblance is a dangerous one to pursue, however, for Hazlitt's published references to Diderot are so brief and vague as to give no indication of what works of the Encyclopædist he had actually read.[25]

[23] "Fine Arts," *Works,* IX, 387–389.
[24] "On the Elgin Marbles," *Works,* IX, 326.
[25] Mr. Howe in his *Life of Hazlitt* (p. 22) says that Hazlitt read the French Encyclopædists during the early years of his philosophical study.

Diderot opens the first chapter of his *Essai sur la Peinture* with the statement that "Nature creates nothing that is incorrect. Every form, whether beautiful or ugly, has its cause; and of all existing creatures there is not one which is not as it must be." [26] He instances the case of a woman who has been blind from childhood and whose eyelid, brow, cheek, even throat and neck have in consequence been modified subtly to accord with the unusual condition. In a hunchback the entire form and even the face are altered by a subtle chain of causes. If all the causes and effects were evident to us, Diderot says, the painter would have no more to do than represent things just as they are. His implication is that a lack of this complete knowledge is the reason for formulation of conventional rules in painting. A crooked nose in nature does not offend us because the adjacent parts are altered to fit or to balance it. But the painter often cannot see these fine relations, and therefore thinks he must correct the model.

The opposition between this view of nature as the object of imitation and the view of Reynolds is obvious. Hazlitt may have been thinking of this passage in Diderot when he says of Hogarth's remarkable power of seeing nature as it is, that in Hogarth's pictures "if the eye squints, the mouth is distorted; every feature acts, and is acted upon by the rest of the face; even the dress and attitude are such as could be proper to no other figure: the whole is under the

I know of no positive proof that Hazlitt read anything by the two editors of the *Encyclopédie*, Diderot and D'Alembert, except the former's contribution to Grimm's *Correspondances* (or that part of it which was contained in either the French or the English abridgment of this work). Of the other contributors to the *Encyclopédie* Hazlitt was familiar with some of the work of Montesquieu, D'Holbach, and, of course, Rousseau.

[26] "La nature ne fait rien d'incorrect. Toute forme, belle ou laide, a sa cause; et, de tous les êtres qui existent, il n'y en a pas un qui ne soit comme il doit être."—Diderot, *Oeuvres*, Paris, 1821. VIII, 407 ff.

influence of one impulse, that of truth and nature." [27] But
Hazlitt finds a further application for this idea. One of his
strongest reasons for objecting to the common belief shared
by Sir Joshua Reynolds and many others, that a painter
should unite in a single beautiful figure excellences which
in nature he has seen only in different forms,[28] is that no
painter—or so Hazlitt thinks—can unite these in an
organic way. He may copy a head from one model and a
form from another; but he will not be able to imagine how
one melts into the other and how each modifies each. Hazlitt also admits that occasionally the painter must do as
Reynolds would constantly have him do, "correct" an
obvious imperfection or irregularity in his model (Hazlitt
does not, though he might, offer Diderot's reason for this,
i. e., man's inability to see and therefore to show in painting the cause of the apparent imperfection), but he contends that, however often the painter is forced to do this,
all the virtue of the picture resides in the other portions:
it is the exactly truthful strokes which make the impression on us and which prove the genius of the painter: the
rest is mere filling in and bridging of gaps, however
skillful.[29]

---

[27] "On the Works of Hogarth," *Lectures on the Comic Writers, Works,*
VIII, 145.
[28] See the following section on *The Ideal.*
[29] "On the Elgin Marbles," *Works,* IX, 331 ff.—In another passage Hazlitt combines a statement of this same idea with a recognition of the
claims of originality. "The plain fact will not constitute a novel," he says;
"there must be the creative spirit to work up all its parts into an em-
bellished picture, and superadd such matters as, although not actually true,
are deducible from that which is, and are relatively consistent; and in proportion to the amount of truth will be the effect and value of the performance." He continues with the remark that fiction is "a transcript from
nature, in which the truth is preserved not *literally*, but *poetically*." In the
Waverley Novels the facts are "elaborated into a more continuous and
imaginative series of impressions, and written out into more passionate
and vivid language" than that in which Sir Walter recorded these facts

There are numerous other parallels between Diderot's ideas of painting and Hazlitt's. Hazlitt's "some one predominant point of view" from which each artist, according to his individual temperament, presents nature, appears in an exaggerated form in Diderot's answer to the question why there occurs such great variation in coloring among artists of what is the same in nature.[30] Hazlitt's discussions of the difficulty of painting expression because of its changing character are very like Diderot's account of the same difficulty in painting flesh.[31] More significant, however, than any specific points are the general similarities of thought and temperament. Both men, in all that they write on art, insist upon the importance of strong feeling, of the *extreme* [32] (but not the *extravagant*), of fidelity to nature, of the careful finishing of all details with perfect truth. Both emphasize the individuality and variety of objects in nature. Diderot writes of *verve* almost as often as Hazlitt does of *gusto,* and they appear to mean much the same thing, that is, intensity.[33] Diderot and the Encyclopædists as a whole disliked and ignored the Middle Ages.[34] Hazlitt did not dislike them, but he stood almost alone among English romantics in not drawing any of his inspiration from mediævalism. He liked a ruined castle in

in his notes ("The Waverley Notes," *New Writings, First Series,* p. 157). Although the topic is ostensibly fiction, Hazlitt was thinking of art in general, as is shown by his use of a comparison from sculpture and by other details in the passage.

[30] Diderot, *op. cit.,* Ch. II, p. 418 ff.

[31] *Ibid.,* p. 425 ff.

[32] For Hazlitt on this, see the following section.

[33] Hazlitt defined gusto in two different ways, once by a passing phrase —"*gusto* or expression"—once as "power or passion defining any object." Both definitions were written in the same year, 1816.—*Works,* IX, 314; I, 77.

[34] Morley remarks that it is for this reason that the Encyclopædists had not the place in romanticism, which "drew its life breath" from the Middle Ages, that they have been thought to have.—John Morley, *Diderot and the Encyclopædists,* I, 346.

the landscape and he liked Sir Walter Scott's novels; but beyond that, the Middle Ages were to him "Gothic" barbarity, much as they were to Pope. The greatest line of divergence, and it is an important one, between the æsthetics of Diderot and of Hazlitt, is in Diderot's very strong tendency to regard art as essentially and first of all moral in purpose. Goethe, who translated part of Diderot's essay on painting into German, criticized this inclination, while acknowledging that in many respects Diderot's æsthetics had opened his eyes.[35] Hazlitt, in the matter of moralistic interpretations of art, was perhaps even farther from Diderot than was Goethe.

The Ideal—Grandeur—Selectiveness—Beauty

It has been seen that in holding the view that art imitates nature Sir Joshua Reynolds identifies nature with the ideal. It is when Hazlitt also begins to discuss the term *ideal* that his most striking difference from Reynolds arises. Reynolds had contended that in order to present the ideal, the unrealized intention of nature, the artist must avoid all extremes and all individuality, and must represent those characteristics which all the objects of a given class have in common—must paint a composite, a "medium" or average form, not a representation of any one model. He even held that there is a single ideal form for every species; that the ideal statue of a man should combine beauties taken from all, should unite in equal parts the activity of the Gladiator, the delicacy of the Greek Apollo, the muscular strength of a Hercules.[36] The *ideal* meant to him, then, the middle or typical in form, a kind of abstracted average.

[35] Werner Leo, *Diderot als Kunstphilosoph*, p. 6 ff.

[36] *Discourse* III. In the fifth *Discourse*, however, he warns the student against the practical dangers of attempting to unite "contrary excellencies."

Hazlitt's conception of the ideal in art was the precise
opposite of this; for he considered it to reside at the extreme instead of at the mean point of any line of truth.
"The ideal," he says in an essay on that subject written
toward the end of his life,[37] "is the abstraction of anything
from all the circumstances that weaken its effect, or lessen
our admiration of it. Or it is filling up the outline of truth
or beauty existing in the mind, so as to leave nothing
wanting or to desire further." Thus far Reynolds would
have agreed. But he goes on: "The principle of the *ideal*
is the satisfaction we have in the contemplation of any
quality or object, which makes us seek to heighten, to prolong, or extend that satisfaction to the utmost." It is the
"highest conceivable degree" of a quality diffused over the
whole of an object. We identify it with "the *divine;* for,
what we imagine of the Gods is pleasure without pain—
power without effort." But we are not justified in supposing, as some do, that it is "brought from another sphere":
we can know nothing of that—"the human form is alone
the image of the divinity." Hazlitt then proceeds more
directly to oppose Reynolds's notion of the ideal as an "abstraction of general nature" or, as Hazlitt says, a "mean or
average proportion between different qualities and faculties, which, instead of carrying any one to the highest point
of perfection or satisfaction, would only neutralize and
damp the impression." [38] In painting one must not try to
produce the *ideal*, therefore, by amalgamating or mud-

---

[37] "The Ideal," *Works*, IX, 429 ff.

[38] Compare with this the second of two essays in *Table-Talk*, "On Certain Inconsistencies in Sir Joshua Reynolds' Discourses," in which Hazlitt
says the same thing even more emphatically: "Ideal expression is not neutral
expression, but extreme expression," and more to the same effect.—*Works*,
VI, 141.—And again: "Instead of its being true in general that the *ideal* is
the middle point, it is to be found in the *extremes;* or, it is carrying any
idea as far as it will go."—"On the Elgin Marbles," *Works*, IX, 339.

dling various things together—the strength of Hercules with the delicacy of Apollo—"but by singling out some one thing or leading quality of an object, and making it the pervading and regulating principle of all the rest. . . . If I see beauty, I do not want to change it for power; if I am struck with power, I am no longer in love with beauty; but I wish to make beauty still more beautiful, power still more powerful, and to pamper and exalt the prevailing impression, whatever it be, till it ends in a dream and a vision of glory." The *ideal* thus becomes "not a negative but a positive thing." [39]

As a rule we think of the ideal as representing a certain class of objects, those which may be said to have "high seriousness." Hazlitt generally associates the ideal with such subjects, though not always. The grounds upon which he refuses the title of *ideal* painter to Hogarth throw some light upon this.[40] Hogarth, he says, has many of the qualities that we associate with the grand or ideal style— beauty, "keeping" in character, general effect and ease of execution, breadth and boldness of manner. What, then, does he lack? He has "an intense feeling and command over the impressions of sense, of habit, of character, and passion, the serious and the comic, in a word, of nature, as it fell within his own observation, or came within the sphere of his actual experience; but he had little power beyond that sphere, or sympathy with that which existed only *in idea.*" There is a mighty world of sense and action, of that which is familiar, "the gross, material, stirring, noisy world of common life" in which Hogarth was a master. But there is a "mightier world, that which exists only

39 "Fine Arts," *Works*, IX, 405.

40 "On the Works of Hogarth," *Lectures on the Comic Writers, Works,* VIII, 142 ff.

in conception and in power, the universe of thought and sentiment, that surrounds and is raised above the ordinary world of reality," in which all things are like not what we ourselves know and feel "in this 'ignorant present' time, but like what they must be in themselves, or in our noblest idea of them." He who stamps these ideas with reality, whether as painter or as poet, is representing the ideal in art. For the ideal appeals to our desire for truth and beauty, to "faculties commensurate with great objects." [41] And again, of the Madonnas of Raphael and Leonardo, Hazlitt says: "This is the *ideal,* passion blended with thought and pointing to distant objects, not debased by grossness, not thwarted by accident, nor weakened by familiarity, but connected with forms and circumstances that give the utmost possible expansion and refinement to the general sentiment." [42]

On the other hand, Hazlitt says, though we usually use the term *ideal* to describe the extreme degree of that which is good or beautiful, yet when the artist selects and paints "a particular form" which expresses most completely and consistently the idea of a given character or quality, no matter whether a high or a low one, he is still painting the *ideal.* A figure of Silenus may be *ideal* as well as a Madonna.[43] That this is the meaning which Hazlitt habitually attaches to the term is clear from many incidental uses which he makes of it. Of Moll Flanders he writes that she carried the love of thieving "to an *ideal* pitch" [44] when she led off a horse from the inn door, though she had nowhere to put it after she had stolen it.[45]

41 *Ibid.,* p. 146.
42 *Ibid.,* p. 148.
43 "The Ideal," *Works,* IX, 433; and "Fine Arts," *Ibid.,* p. 405.
44 "Wilson's Life and Times of Daniel Defoe," *Works,* X, 381.
45 In one essay, however, that "On the Picturesque and Ideal" in *Table-*

The opposition of Hazlitt and Reynolds on this point is the opposition of a pluralistic to a monistic philosophy, and of a romantic to a classic taste. Reynolds's *ideal* finds significance not in the multiplicity of nature, but in the discovery of a more unifying, simplifying, generalizing principle in which alone meaning resides, the apparent multiplicity of the universe being only the aggregate of imperfections. To the pluralistic view of Hazlitt, on the other hand, significance resides and is to be sought in the very differences themselves between individual objects. We increase our understanding, as he sees it, not by generalizing but by distinguishing. The romantic aspect of this theory lies in its emphasis upon the individual instead of the class, and in its finding the *ideal* at the extreme point of any line of truth instead of at the mean point.

Talk, Hazlitt presents a quite different view of the whole subject, a view in which he partly goes over to Sir Joshua's side. The *picturesque* is here defined as that which stands out strikingly to the eye, which tends often toward the fantastic and grotesque, and which has a *decided* character. The *ideal,* on the contrary, answers to a preconceived idea in the mind, to a desire for love and beauty (here the idea is the same as that expressed in the lecture on Hogarth). Rubens's landscapes are picturesque, Claude's are ideal: for "Rubens is always in extremes: Claude in the middle. Rubens carries some one peculiar quality or feature of nature to the utmost verge of probability: Claude balances and harmonizes different forms and masses with laboured delicacy, so that nothing falls short, no one thing overpowers another." The *ideal* is "the height of the pleasing, that which satisfies and accords with the inmost longing of the soul": the picturesque is merely "a sharper and bolder impression of reality." The picturesque is *truth,* and appeals to sense and understanding; the ideal is *good,* and appeals to the will and affections: it is "the infinite with respect to human capacities and wishes."—*Works,* VI, 317 ff.—In this passage it will be noted that Hazlitt uses in passing Reynolds's notion (which he everywhere else opposes) of the ideal as "the middle." The identification of the *ideal* with the will and affections here is perhaps a trace of Coleridge's influence. Altogether the passage contains interesting distinctions and would be important for our account of Hazlitt's theory if it were not so clear that this is only an *occasional* definition. In passages written both before and after this essay he returns invariably to the view which has already been discussed, to the definition of the *ideal* as the carrying of an idea "as far as it will go."

Closely related to Sir Joshua Reynolds's theory of the ideal in painting is his belief that to achieve the grand style an artist should avoid detail as far as possible. The whole beauty and grandeur of art consists in "being able to get above all singular forms, local customs, particularities, and details of every kind." [46] One of the chief dangers against which students of painting should be warned is that of too great minuteness. It is not possible to avoid detail altogether, for the painter must impart "an air of truth" to his work; [47] the portrait painter in particular has to make concessions in this direction, since he is after all paid for producing a likeness. In a later *Discourse* [48] Reynolds makes a less dogmatic and more reasonable statement on this point. The painter's object, he says, is to express his subject "*as a whole*," and all particularity of detail which does not contribute to this end is mischievous. In ordinary life the impression which is made upon our mind even by things familiar to us is "seldom more than their general effect"; beyond this we do not look. Since this is the nature of man's mind, it should also be the nature of art, which must always "express what is congenial and natural to the mind of man, and what gives him by reflection his own mode of conceiving."

This statement is of peculiar interest with regard to Hazlitt, for it starts with the same premise as his and yet reaches a contrary conclusion. One of Hazlitt's favorite contentions, it will be recalled,[49] is that all our ideas are general and abstract because of our inability to perceive or to know all about any single object in nature. But our advance in knowledge consists in making these general

[46] *Discourse* III.
[47] *Discourse* IV.
[48] *Discourse* XI.
[49] See p. 24 ff., above.

ideas by degrees less general and more particular; or, in other words, it consists in the process of *discrimination*. The great artist is one who sees farther into his subject than others. A certain scene may convey to a landscape painter a feeling or impression unlike that conveyed by any other scene. His greatness consists in his recognizing the distinct feeling and in his power to discover those specific elements in the scene which produce its special or characteristic quality. This of necessity involves an extraordinary perceptiveness and an accurate representation of individual details in their relation to each other. Thus Hazlitt's philosophical doctrine of abstract ideas, his pluralistic point of view, his disagreement with Sir Joshua Reynolds's theory, his complaint against the English school of painters for their lack of "finishing" and of details, are all manifestations of a consistent line of thought.

In criticizing Reynolds's conception of grandeur Hazlitt contends that the grand style consists neither in giving nor in avoiding details but in something quite different from both. "Any one may avoid the details. So far, there is no difference between the *Cartoons,* and a common sign-painting." But grandeur "consists in giving the larger masses and proportions with truth;—this does not prevent giving the smaller ones too." The utmost grandeur is perfectly compatible with minuteness and delicacy, a fact which is perfectly proved for all time, Hazlitt feels, by the example of the Elgin Marbles.[50] These are finished to the utmost detail; a single fingernail is done as perfectly as a whole figure. The exact gradations by which one part of a form melts into another are perfectly represented. Yet they are as a whole the grandest examples we know of ancient sculpture. It is true that the mechanical imitation of

50 "Fine Arts," *Works,* IX, 402.

individual objects does not of itself produce beauty or grandeur. But it is not therefore to be inferred that art consists in *not* imitating individual nature.[51]

In his theory of art, however, as Mr. Chase points out,[52] Hazlitt fails to recognize adequately the significance of the principle of selection. He takes for granted that the artist must be selective: the realistic Dutch painters he thought were inferior to the great Italians partly from their not selecting the finest subjects; the Elgin Marbles, on the other hand, he conceives to have been done from living models selected from among the finest figures in nature. The artist's prerogative of selecting and combining, of arranging his groups, is assumed. More than this too is assumed. For in speaking of the truly great or "historical" in portraits, Hazlitt says that success comes with seizing "the predominant form or expression, and preserving it with truth throughout every part. It is representing the individual under one consistent, probable, and striking view; or shewing the different features, muscles, etc. in one action and modified by one principle." [53] This must, one would suppose, imply a selectiveness not only of the subject itself but also of certain details within the subject. Yet Hazlitt never quite takes up the question from this angle, and never appears to ask himself whether the artist under these circumstances does in fact produce an "exact and wonderful facsimile of nature," or whether the artist is not altering the multiplicity of nature by his "one consistent and striking view." [54] Hazlitt recognized, too,

[51] "On the Imitation of Nature," *Works*, XI, 216 ff.
[52] S. P. Chase, *op. cit.*, p. 190 ff.
[53] "On the Imitation of Nature," *Works*, XI, 221.
[54] This is not strictly true. In an essay on "Originality" (*Works*, IX, 423 ff.) Hazlitt objects to the common assumption that the object and our image of it are the same. This error, he says, is the reason that we fail often to understand originality as possible in an artist without his being

though he appears not to have been aware of its bearing
upon his theory of imitation, the necessity for individuality in the great artist. In a criticism of Lucien Buonaparte's poetry he finds that primarily the work is not great
because "the whole wants character: it does not bear the
stamp of the same presiding mind." [55] Hazlitt thus constantly assumed the selectiveness of art without in general
attempting to discuss it or to make it a part of his theory.[56]

There were, in fact, times when Hazlitt was unable to
accept or to be satisfied with the views of art which he prevailingly owned, just as there were in his philosophy
moments when he was drawn a little in the direction of
Platonism.

Because the human mind is incapable of comprehending
multiplicity and tends therefore inevitably to reduce phenomena to unity, the attempt intellectually to preserve the
opposite aim is most arduous, and is, one would think, certain to have its relapses. This does not mean that one view
is more demonstrably—or even more probably—true than
the other. Man's tendency to find singleness of meaning in
multiplicity of phenomena may indeed exist because the
ultimate reality is unity; but it may equally well exist only
because of man's limited and finite mind. Hazlitt, though
he chose to believe the latter, could not escape the natural
tendency of human thought. He expresses himself at one
point in his discussion of Sir Joshua's theories as being

untrue to nature. His explanation here is adequate. But the fact remains
that everywhere else in his discussions of art and imitation Hazlitt leaves
this link in the chain missing. One cannot avoid the conclusion that though
he was thus capable of thinking out the point, he did not incorporate it
into his theory of art as a whole.

[55] "Charlemagne: ou l'Eglise Delivrée," *Works*, XI, 230.

[56] This is to be accounted for in part by the fact that the established
tradition against which Hazlitt was in protest made so much of selectiveness, in its "corrective" attitude toward nature.

somewhat puzzled over the question of beauty. It is, he
thinks, "the principle of affinity between different forms,
or their gradual conversion into each other." It depends
not solely upon custom or fashion, or even association, as
Sir Joshua, with some doubts however, maintained. Hazlitt, at least for the moment, believes that there is a
principle of symmetry or harmony existing outside and independent of man, which constitutes intrinsic beauty.[57]
One species of object is in itself more beautiful than another: the Greek physiognomy, from the fine interrelation
of its lines and curves, is intrinsically more beautiful than
the African.[58] In the end he confesses that "on this subject of beauty, we are half-disposed to fall into the mysticism of Raphael Mengs, who had some notion about a
principle of *universal harmony,* if we did not dread the
censure of an eminent critic." [59] This is very Platonic indeed; for in the beginning of his *Reflections upon Beauty
and Taste in Painting* Mengs says: "Since perfection is not
allotted to mankind, and is only to be found in God, and
as nothing is comprehensible to our nature except that
which falls under the conviction of the senses; thus the
Omnipotent has thought fit to imprint a visible *Idea* of
that perfection, which is what we call Beauty." Beauty is,
in fact, the "soul of matter." Its basis is uniformity: whence
a single pure color and a circle are the most beautiful objects in color and form.[60]

[57] "On the Elgin Marbles," *Works,* IX, 345–346.
[58] Hazlitt appears to accept here without discussion Burke's distinction
between the sublime and the beautiful as founded in the sense of danger
and the social sense respectively. In Hazlitt's version of the distinction, the
sublime creates a feeling of awe out of images of power or magnitude, while
the beautiful "melts the heart" by images which he scarcely attempts to
analyze.
[59] "The Ideal," *Works,* XI, 230.
[60] Anthony Raphael Mengs, *Works.* An English translation from the

To this extreme Hazlitt was only "half-inclined." He never arrived at any final conclusion on the subject.

Genius

In discussing Hazlitt's theory of imitation something has been said of nature as the object of imitation, and something also, largely by implication, of genius. After all, if one has once succeeded in saying what art is, the definition of the artist should be an obvious enough corollary. Nevertheless in Hazlitt's day (and even to some degree in our own) discussions upon the constitution of genius often approach the problems of art from a different angle—usually a more purely psychological one. What Hazlitt has to say upon this subject therefore requires some separate account.

Hazlitt stands between the extreme "common-sense" belief that genius consists in the infinite capacity for taking pains, which is on the whole Sir Joshua's view,[61] and the opposite conception of genius as bringer of the sacred fire of truth from heaven. On the whole, Hazlitt tends to approach this latter extreme as nearly as his tacit scepticism will allow. Of a landscape by Claude he says that its union of truth and beauty "suggests the feeling of immortality"; [62] indeed in any great gallery of pictures we "seem identified with the permanent forms of things." [63] The works of genius *seem*, that is, to bring us in touch with truth that is beyond the reach of human reason. Whether

Italian, published in London, 1796. Quotations are from the first three chapters of the *Reflections*.

[61] On this, as on other points, however, Reynolds's opinions were not consistent. His later *Discourses* in particular tend to recognize the existence of a *gift* in the artist.

[62] "Pictures at Wilton, Stourhead, etc.," *Picture Galleries in England, Works*, IX, 57.

[63] "Mr. Angerstein's Collection," *Ibid.*, p. 7.

this is more than seeming Hazlitt will not venture to say. Even if it is illusory, the ability of genius to conceive such illusion, like the power of man to invent religion if it has no extra-human actuality, is in itself worthy of reverence.

On a more strictly human plane, Hazlitt defined genius as an involuntary power—and therefore a power not to be acquired by study, as Sir Joshua held—of seeing nature "differently from others, and yet as it is in itself": it is the discovery of "new and valuable truth." [64] Or, in more formal terms, "genius is the power which equalizes or identifies the imagination with the reality or with nature." [65] As opposed to mere taste, which rests upon fine sensibility, genius is the result of an active power—of the highest degree of power—both of feeling and of invention.[66] "Invention" does not involve a departure from nature: it is "little more than the fertility of a teeming brain." If the invention were not "true," that is, founded "in our consciousness or experience," we should greet it not as a discovery but as pure nonsense.[67] Genius is identified by Hazlitt almost always with originality as "some strong quality in the mind, answering to and bringing out some new and striking quality in nature." Like a glow-worm, it "discloses a little circle of gorgeous light in the twilight of obscurity, in the night of intellect, that surrounds it." [68] A work shows genius in proportion as it gives us what is to be found nowhere else.[69] But this can be given only by one

[64] "On Genius and Common Sense," *Table-Talk, Works,* VI, 46; and "The Indian Jugglers," *Ibid.,* p. 84.
[65] "Madame Pasta and Mademoiselle Mars," *Plain Speaker, Works,* VII, 334.
[66] "Why the Arts are not Progressive," *Round Table, Works,* I, 164.
[67] "Originality," *Works,* IX, 428.
[68] "On Genius and Common Sense," *Table-Talk, Works,* VI, 42–43.
[69] Wordsworth had much the same idea. The proof of genius, he says in the "Essay Supplementary to the Preface" of the *Lyrical Ballads,* is "the

whose eye is always intent on nature and who is ever
"brooding over 'beauty, rendered still more beautiful' by
the exquisite feeling with which it is contemplated." [70]
That which stamps the character of genius on works of art
more than anything else is a certain "intuitive perception
of the hidden analogies of things," an "instinct of the
imagination," which works unconsciously, "like nature,"
from a kind of inspiration.[71] The essence of genius is indeed an instinctive yearning after truth and an approxi-
mation towards it "before it is acknowledged by others,
and almost before the mind itself knows what it is." [72]

Occasionally Hazlitt pondered another idea of genius,
which may or may not have been suggested to him by the
painter Northcote. It is interesting as being a theory that
is today widely held by psychologists. In one of the *Conversations of Northcote* the old painter remarks [73] that it
is only defects in other directions that make for distinction
as an artist: that "we only work out our way to excellence
by being imprisoned in defects." Art, he says, requires
such a long apprenticeship, so much self-denial, that a man
will submit to it only when easier means of escaping obscurity fail. Wealth, or great popularity or happiness in

act of doing well what is worthy to be done, and what was never done before." In the fine arts the only infallible sign of genius is "the widening
the sphere of human sensibility, for the delight, honour, and benefit of
human nature."

70 "On Genius and Originality," *Works*, XI, 210–212.

71 "On the English Novelists," *Lectures on the Comic Writers, Works,*
VIII, 109. Also *Works*, X, 29.

72 "Originality," *Works*, IX, 428.

73 It should be noted that in these *Conversations* the ideas attributed to
Northcote were by no means always his. Much of the dialogue is admittedly
of Hazlitt's own invention: witness, for this, Hazlitt's own preliminary
statement to the volume, and the fact that, throughout, all the best remarks (many with a definitely Hazlittean flavor) are put into Northcote's
mouth.—See also Howe's *Life*, pp. 410–411.

youth is therefore enough usually to prevent a man's becoming a great painter. Hazlitt in his own person demurs
a little: he ventures the opinion that where there is "a
strong turn for anything" the application required for its
development, though great, brings with it enough satisfaction to make it comparatively easy. Northcote "turned
short round" upon him and said, "Then you admit original genius?" "Waiving that," Hazlitt replies, "and not in-
quiring how the inclination comes, but early in life a fond-
ness, a passion for a certain pursuit is imbibed; the mind
is haunted by this object, it cannot rest without it (any
more than the body without food), it becomes the strongest
feeling we have, and then, I think, the most intense application follows naturally; . . . the most unremitting application without this is forced and of no use; and where
this original bias exists, no other motive is required." [74]
But much earlier than this, in an essay "On the Causes of
Methodism" Hazlitt himself accounts for the commonly
ridiculed "pining, puritanical, poverty-struck" appearance
of poets, authors, and artists in general, not from external
poverty, as has been supposed, but "perhaps" from the fact
that their being poets and artists is owing to their "original
poverty of spirit and weakness of constitution." For the
most part, he says, "those who are dissatisfied with themselves, will seek to go out of themselves into an ideal
world. Persons in strong health and spirits, who take
plenty of air and exercise, who are 'in favour with their
stars,' and have a thorough relish of the good things of
this life, seldom devote themselves in despair to religion
or the Muses. Sedentary, nervous, hypochondriacal people,
on the contrary, are forced, for want of an appetite for the

[74] "Conversation the Fifth," *Works,* VI, 360–361.

real and substantial, to look out for a more airy food and speculative comforts." [75]

This is an extremely modern view. It is uttered by Hazlitt rather casually in the midst of his account of the thwarted, feeble, pathetic creatures that most Methodists were in his day. Few would now deny that there is something in it, though as a complete theory it is unwelcome to those who care seriously for any of the arts. Nor does it represent Hazlitt's main theory, as we have seen; but it is interesting as an instance of a kind of psychological insight not common in his day. The art and genius that Hazlitt admires most is, however, the kind least likely to have had this origin. The universal, unimpeded flow of sympathy in Shakespeare and (in an entirely different degree) in Scott, the utter soundness in strength and health of feeling that seems to glow through their works and through those of Titian in painting do not in the least seem like the result of thwarted personalities. It is rather as if their very freedom as individuals gave them the power of looking "beyond themselves to others," of understanding "nature" by their unimpeded sympathy in precisely the way that constitutes *genius* as Hazlitt elsewhere describes it. The two views of *genius* are, in fact, not contradictory, but may be united in varying proportions within the work of the same individuals. But Hazlitt never brings them together.

"Why the Arts Are Not Progressive"

One achievement of criticism in the early nineteenth century was its setting finally to rest the illusion of an advance in the progress of art comparable to that in scientific knowledge. The presumption of much English criticism

[75] *Round Table, Works,* I, 58.

from the time of the Restoration, as of French in the preceding years, was that we had now come to an age of enlightenment in the arts; that crudeness and barbarity had been pruned away, yet that we had the advantage of the best of our predecessors' achievements to use as models and to improve upon. Hence we might be supposed to see either already flourishing, or—in an art like that of historical painting of which this could not possibly be claimed —upon the very threshold of florescence, the topmost glories which the arts had ever reached. This was essentially Sir Joshua Reynolds's view. With all his enthusiasm for Michelangelo and Raphael, and for ancient sculpture, his emphasis upon the importance of imitating the great masters derives from the conviction that only thus can the present generation of painters fulfill their destiny and, as his contemporaries in other arts were doing, learn to excel their masters.[76]

Hazlitt had at least as much to do as any other single writer with rendering this position forever untenable, though the view had by no means remained unchallenged until his day. The logical flaw underlying this assumption of the progressiveness of art was brought out as early as 1694 in William Wotton's *Reflections upon Ancient and Modern Learning,* and was developed in French thought by the Abbé Du Bos.[77] Hazlitt speaks in familiar terms of the essays of Sir William Temple, in which already the steady historical advance of the arts was questioned; whether he had read Du Bos or Wotton we do not know. But he need have gone no further than to Johnson's *Rasselas,* which of course he knew, to encounter the obser-

[76] It is true, the contrary opinion was also held (often by the same persons who held this one), that the ancients are supreme and can only be feebly imitated by us.

[77] A. Bosker, *Literary Criticism in the Age of Johnson,* p. 50 ff.

vation that as a rule the most ancient poets of a nation are considered the best, with the suggested explanation that other kinds of knowledge are gradual acquisitions, whereas poetry is "a gift conferred at once." [78]

Hazlitt in a sense does little more than elaborate this remark of Johnson's; but he does so at length and in a systematic fashion, so that it becomes an integral part of his theory of art as it was not with the earlier writers. The arts, he says in a discussion of this subject in one of the *Round Table* papers, as they are not mechanical, nor reducible to rule, nor capable of demonstration, cannot reasonably be expected to attain a progressive degree of perfection as can science; and neither the study of the antique, nor the formation of academies and the distribution of prizes will enable us to excel our predecessors. For genius cannot be taught: it springs up we know not how; and the material upon which genius works is nature, which does not change. Hazlitt says, as Johnson did, that the greatest geniuses in poetry, painting, and sculpture appeared "soon after the birth of these arts" in their respective civilizations. The source of art lies in what we know and see and feel most intimately. Man's feelings three thousand years ago were as they are now, and the imagination of genius could penetrate the heart then as well as now.[79] Science is based on the accumulation of knowledge, so that *without increasing the power of mind* we can yet build up increasing knowledge. But art depends upon the "original force of capacity, and degree of attention. . . ." [80]

This too, like the rest of Hazlitt's theory of art, falls into

---

[78] *Ibid.*, p. 54; and *Rasselas*, Chapter 10.
[79] "Why the Arts are not Progressive," *Works*, I, 160 ff.
[80] "Why the Arts are not Progressive," *Works*, IX, 489–490 (Appendix I).

place within the general outlines of his philosophy; and it may be well to pause here for a moment to resume that thread. As was said earlier, Hazlitt owed a great deal to Rousseau's philosophy of *feeling*. But the distinction cannot be too clearly drawn between Rousseau's apotheosis of feeling and Hazlitt's simple acceptance of it as the fundamental driving force of human nature. Such justice as may be granted to some of the modern strictures upon Rousseau's philosophy as a disintegrating force in civilization—those voiced by the recently deflated American Humanists, for example [81]—fails to apply, in anything like the same degree at least, to Hazlitt. For the idealization of feeling and the "natural man" is a bubble thoroughly pricked by our increased knowledge of the life and customs of primitive man as well as by the rise of Darwinist evolutionary theories and their later consequents. Any consistent attempt to follow Rousseau's return to nature as a way of life is inconceivable now, its results would so obviously be a far worse than "natural" chaos: the tangle of man's troubles cannot be cut as easily as Rousseau supposed. But Hazlitt's philosophy of feeling does not in the same way block the avenues of possible development. To postulate emotion as the primary motive of man's action *as a fact* is quite different from postulating it *as an intrinsic value*. If feeling is to be worshiped for its own sake, then reason either cannot or else should not be accepted as a guide to action. But to believe with Hazlitt that—though reason may be the highest gift conferred on man, the topmost excellence that sets him apart from the beasts—his actions are yet fundamentally determined by feeling rather than by reason—to believe this is to have a conception that is quite

[81] See Irving Babbitt's *Rousseau and Romanticism* for the strongest exposition of this view of the romantic writers.

in tune with the progress of biological science since Hazlitt's day, and that admits also the possible development of man's reason more and more as an aid in working out his destiny.

For all his enthusiastic devotion to Rousseau, Hazlitt never shows himself the implicit follower of the Frenchman that his ebullient friend the painter Haydon, for example, was. Writing of the great Italians Haydon on one occasion said: "Raphael, Correggio, Michael Angelo, and Julio Romano's powers were adequate to elevate man to his original essence, and by rejecting all the accidents of disease and degeneration which have degraded his being, restored him to his essential beauty, and his essential essence." [82] In Hazlitt there was none of this idealization of the "natural man." Indeed, Hazlitt's philosophy, and his temperament as reflected in his philosophy preserved him from a fault into which Rousseau at one extreme and Coleridge at the other both fell—the confusion of fact with feeling. Coleridge's whole life is a witness to this confusion.[83] As for Rousseau, it is characteristic of him that, having undertaken to write upon the "Origin of Inequality amongst Mankind," a subject proposed for discussion by the Academy of Dijon, he should have set off for the country with his mistress and have buried himself each day alone, without the presence of a single human being, in the forest of St. Germain, where he "sought and found the picture of those primitive times," of which he "boldly sketched the history." [84]

[82] B. R. Haydon, *Correspondence and Table-Talk*, II, 91.

[83] It would take some time to substantiate this in detail. But one cannot, I think, have read through Coleridge's letters and observed there and elsewhere in his works the operation of his famous inaccuracy in relation to the facts of his life, without acceding to the statement.

[84] Rousseau's *Confessions* (Everyman ed.), II, 39.

As compared with these—the man who writes history
out of his inner consciousness, and the man who, as
Mr. Shawcross says, considers the vividness of any experience as the measure of its truth [85]—although for other
reasons he is not as great as either of them, Hazlitt pre-
serves a nice balance: he is neither sentimentalist nor mystic, nor rationalist either—but represents the realistic
tradition arising perhaps out of eighteenth-century "common sense" but broadened and deepened in his day under
the influence of a changing world.

Taste—Form

Hazlitt's discussion of *taste* is peculiarly eighteenth-
century in tone. It is also peculiarly inconclusive. Yet it
shows him fitting nineteenth-century conceptions into
eighteenth-century phraseology. In three short essays on the
subject, two of them contributed to the *Edinburgh Review*
in 1818 and 1819,[86] he makes the statement that taste is
"nothing but sensibility to the different degrees and kinds of
excellence in the works of art or nature." The emphasis of a
person of taste should be upon the "beauties" rather than
the "blemishes" of a work. Any one is capable of finding out
that Bohemia has no sea-coast, and no doubt Shakespeare's
supposing that it had constitutes a "blemish." But it requires no taste to point this out. The essence of taste is in
sympathy: it consists in the power of perceiving and being
moved by that which genius has had the power to produce.
It is therefore a positive, not a negative quality. But Hazlitt
runs into the usual dilemma on the question of taste.
Though its basis is in feeling, he does not admit that one
man's feeling has the same validity as another's. "The ulti-

[85] Pp. 25–26, above.
[86] "Thoughts on Taste," *Works*, XI, 450 ff.

mate and only conclusive proof of taste" is "enthusiasm," he says at one point; [87] and yet only a few pages further on [88] he replies to the rhetorical question "whether mere extravagance and enthusiasm are proofs of taste," that they are not, "where they are without reason and knowledge." Not "mere sensibility," but "sensibility to real excellence" constitutes taste. The highest taste is sensible to the greatest beauties; the most catholic taste to the greatest variety of excellence. But the question of what is real excellence, and who is to be the judge of it, Hazlitt does not clearly formulate. His practical statement on this point is that "to agree with the greatest number of good judges, is to be in the right; and good judges are persons of natural sensibility and acquired knowledge." Yet even this he does not hold without exception. For there is more appreciation in France—and by more judges, good ones in their way—of Racine and Molière, than there is in England of Shakespeare; and yet Hazlitt is sure that Shakespeare is greater than Racine or Molière.

On the whole Hazlitt's discussion of this subject is very like the attitude of those eighteenth-century critics who set up "taste" in opposition to "common sense." They, like him, considered both taste and genius as native qualities which might be improved by cultivation. This was the view of Goldsmith, that taste is "composed of Nature improved by Art; of Feeling tutored by Instruction." [89] In the further step of finding the criteria of what is excellent in the opinions of the general body of those qualified to

[87] *Ibid.,* p. 454.

[88] *Ibid.,* p. 457. This and the above occur in separate essays, the first published in October, 1818, this in July, 1819. But they were intended as a continuous discussion of the same question, and the interval between the publication of them does not necessarily represent a lapse of time in the writing.

[89] Bosker, *op. cit.,* p. 147.

judge, Hazlitt's opinion resembles that of Hugh Blair in
one of his lectures.[90] But in thus setting up a kind of public opinion as the final arbiter of taste, Hazlitt was no intellectual democrat. "Taste becomes grosser, the more it is
diffused," he remarks on one occasion. It is not popularity
that determines the excellence of a work of art; those only
are qualified to judge who are endowed with an exceptional degree of sensibility and who have cultivated it by
fixed attention to and long study of art and nature. And
it is only after generations have passed and we find that
people of taste still admire an old work—only then that we
can be sure that it possesses true greatness: a man of even
the "most refined taste" cannot judge with certainty of
contemporary works.

Hazlitt's clearest attempt to pick a way between the two
extremes of rational judgement and personal preference
as a basis for taste in art is made in an essay published now
with the other two on "Taste" as "The Same Subject Continued," but apparently never printed during Hazlitt's
life time. Here he undertakes to show that merely "because there is no dogmatic or bigoted standard of taste, like
a formula of faith, which whoever does not believe without
doubt he shall be damned everlastingly," it does not follow that there is no standard whatever. For although not
all persons receive pleasure from the same things, yet it is
observable that certain things are more apt to please than
others, that some objects please more generally or more
permanently, some give most pleasure to those who have
most studied the subject, some please one nation more than

90 Bosker, *op. cit.*, pp. 160–161. There is no certain evidence, however, of
Hazlitt's having read Blair's *Lectures*, and the idea was current among
many writers. Much the same is to be found in Johnson. In fact it was
little different from the current "common-sense" view of that day—or any
other.

another. It would be difficult, he thinks, to force all these into a single law or system; yet it is not true that they are entirely accidental or without any principle or cause whatever. From a consideration of all these elements, as well as from knowing what over a period of time the best judges have felt, and what we ourselves feel, we may arrive at an approximate though not absolute standard of taste.[91] But this last, *what we ourselves feel,* is in the end the most important basis of judgement. The common fault, if we fail to depend on this, is that we shall judge on the basis of "a commonplace, a preconception, the moulds of the judgement preoccupied by certain assumptions of degrees and classes of excellence, instead of judging from the true and genuine impressions of things": that is, we shall assume, for example, as did so many learned judges of Hazlitt's day, that Raphael was a greater painter than Titian, because we are accustomed to assume the superiority of the "historical" *genre* over the portrait, regardless whether the *impression actually made* upon the beholder is greater or not.[92]

On the point raised by this illustration, that is, on the relative value of different *genres,* Hazlitt tends to accept the opinion of Reynolds that "history" painting is the highest aim for a painter. In the seventh chapter of his *Notes of a Journey through France and Italy* [93] he speaks of the imitation of nature "which belongs to painting in general" and of expression, which is "giving the soul of nature," and which "belongs more particularly to history

[91] The only way to arrive at an absolute standard, he says, would be by knowing, not what *does* but what *would* please universally, "supposing all men to have paid an equal attention to any subject and to have an equal relish for it."
[92] *Ibid.,* p. 461.
[93] *Works,* IX, 130.

painting." This is a statement made in passing, the real topic here being the faults of French art. But he makes the same assumption elsewhere. On the other hand he cannot be said to hold this view with any enthusiasm, perhaps not even with much conviction. Quite as often as remarks like this we meet others spoken, as a rule, more obviously from his own person. In *The Picture Galleries of England*,[94] after describing at length one of his favorite paintings, "Jacob's Dream," by Rembrandt, he goes on briefly to others, by Hobbema and Jacob van Ruysdael: "Is not this a sad anticlimax . . . ? We do not know: and we should care as little, could we but paint either of the pictures. . . . If a picture is admirable in its kind, we do not give ourselves much trouble about the subject." This is a cardinal point with Hazlitt: that there are different kinds of excellence, and that each must be judged according to its own kind.

Hazlitt often appears, like most other romantics, to neglect the element of form in art. It is true that he had little interest in design as such. But for organic form, to which, however, he did not apply that name as Coleridge did, he had a strong sense. Frequently he emphasized, like Diderot, the importance of seeing the whole as constituted by closely related parts, each modifying each.[95] Objects in nature, he says, conform not only to a class but to themselves as well, by a certain "symmetry of parts, a principle of proportion, gradation, harmony." [96] The painter can succeed only by selecting and embodying "some one view of nature." This kind of form, which comes from the unity of the artist's

[94] "The Dulwich Gallery," *Works*, IX, 22.
[95] For further comments of Diderot on this point see Diderot, *op. cit.*, p. 416.
[96] "On Beauty," *Round Table*, *Works*, I, 68.

original vision of his subject, is the foundation of all the more superficial elements of form—pattern in repetition or balanced design. Hazlitt has little interest and little faith in the attempts to codify rules by which this unity is achieved; but that he considers the basic unity of a composition as essential to its effect is made clear by all that he says on the subject of imitation and the ideal. Here too his fundamental disagreement with Reynolds appears, even though both speak for the same kind of unity. Reynolds remarks that painting is an instance of the superiority of mind over matter because it "contracts into one whole what nature has made multifarious." [97] With Hazlitt this was rather a sign of the limitation of man's comprehension of nature than a sign of his superiority over it.

[97] *Discourse* XI.

III

Hazlitt's

APPLICATION OF ÆSTHETIC THEORY TO LITERATURE

Sources—Hazlitt and Coleridge

THE question of Hazlitt's intellectual debts, to his contemporaries and his predecessors as well, is no simple one. It is significant that, thoroughgoing romanticist as he in many respects was, his most frequent quotations on theoretical aspects of the arts are from such accepted eighteenth-century fountains of wisdom as Horace's *Ars Poetica,* which he seems to have had practically by heart,[1] and Pope's *Essay on Criticism.* A great deal of Hazlitt's thinking, in fact, was cast in eighteenth-century classical moulds. Oddly enough, though in politics Hazlitt felt constrained to throw over the friendship of all those who differed from him (especially, of course, those who had once shared his sympathy for the French Revolution) yet he seems to have had little impulse to do the same outside of politics. In philosophy, it is true, he had a great dislike for Helvétius and Condillac, and a good deal—only half confessed—for Locke. But he had great respect for Hume, and may quite as well have owed to him as to Rousseau the formulation of his belief that "reason is, and ought to be, only the slave of the passions." (The words are Hume's and

---

[1] He quotes as a rule from the Latin, but occasionally also from the English translation of Roscommon.

not Hazlitt's—or Rousseau's, as one might suppose them.) Indeed, Hazlitt tended to accept the old formulas whenever he could, but to inject, consciously or not, new meaning into them.

Hazlitt's breadth of taste in literature has often been remarked: the fact that with all his enthusiasm for the romantic Elizabethans he was still able to see—as Wordsworth and Coleridge, and indeed most of the romanticists, were not—the greatness of Dryden and Pope and Dr. Johnson. The fact perhaps is, as has been already suggested, that Hazlitt was himself first of all a product of eighteenth-century "common sense." His attachment in early youth to the *Tatler* and the *Spectator* and all their train, to the novelists, Fielding, Richardson, Smollett, to Pope—this attachment simply remained as a fundamental part of his thought throughout his life. What he himself told Coleridge upon one occasion, that he had not changed his opinions since he was sixteen, was quite true: he had grown broader in knowledge and appreciation, had found out the greatness of Shakespeare and the other old writers, had seen and loved and tried to paint pictures, had found a deeper significance in art and life; but he had not thrown anything away. He had not had to react against his past as Coleridge did, nor to retire from it into himself like Wordsworth. The reading of Rousseau opened new horizons to him, but did not close the old ones. In this he presents the greatest contrast to Coleridge. Granting the continuity of much of Coleridge's thought, there was yet in him such a strong need to escape from himself that the path of his life seems strewn with dead selves: the reading of Bowles's sonnets, for instance, reduced Coleridge's first poetic self to ashes. But in Hazlitt there were no revolutions. Even his violent politics, his sympathy with the

French Revolution and his unvarying condemnation of England's part in the Napoleonic wars were a natural enough development from the ideas implanted in his childhood by a father who had, like Priestley, opposed the war with America. Thus Hazlitt had taken the eighteenth century with him when he entered the nineteenth.

So it was in his conception of nature, and in his use of the formula that art must imitate nature, which, despite the romantic "return to nature," was not a romanticist formula. So also we find him speaking of "beauties" in pictures or poetry as isolated bits, in a distinctly old-fashioned manner, as well as quoting Horace and Pope as authorities on poetry. Reynolds's *Discourses*, as we have seen, Burke's *Essay on the Sublime and Beautiful*, the criticism of Dryden, Addison, Dr. Johnson—though he voiced more disagreement with these than with Pope and Horace—were none of them without great influence upon his thought.

But the question of Hazlitt's relation to Coleridge requires a somewhat more minute inspection. As has already been remarked,[2] writers on either Hazlitt or Coleridge have regularly assumed, if they mention the existence of general principles in Hazlitt's criticism at all, that he derived them as a whole from Coleridge. That this could not be altogether true must already have become apparent in view of Hazlitt's interest in the æsthetic problems raised by the criticism of painting—a subject with which Coleridge was comparatively unfamiliar, and which unquestionably furnished some points of view which Hazlitt carried over into his literary criticism. Nor could it be entirely true, apart from the question of painting, because of what has been shown of their philosophical opposition. Coleridge the neo-

[2] Introduction, p. 4.

Platonic idealist and Hazlitt the realist could not have written criticism based upon the same postulates. This is not to deny that Hazlitt was in some respects deeply indebted to Coleridge, as he himself freely admitted. At the end of his lecture on "The Living Poets" he remarks that Coleridge is "the only person from whom I ever learnt anything." [3] There is something of exaggeration, certainly, in this. But in the essay "On Reading Old Books" he says: "I believe I may date my insight into the mysteries of poetry from the commencement of my acquaintance with the authors of the *Lyrical Ballads;* at least, my discrimination of the higher sorts—not my predilection for such writers as Goldsmith or Pope." [4] On the other hand upon a different occasion he wrote that he had never learned much about Shakespeare and Milton from Coleridge or Wordsworth because he had never heard either say much about them.[5] These are all utterances dropped incidentally on the way to other things. They are not, obviously, very reassuring in their consistency. The main situation of Hazlitt's intellectual relationship to Coleridge, however, is fairly clear on other evidence, though on some specific points relating to his indebtedness it is impossible to arrive at positive conclusions. The facts come to this: Hazlitt was brought up mainly on eighteenth-century literature. But before he met Coleridge he had become an ardent student of philosophy, was well read in the work of the materialists and was already opposed to it. He had read Berkeley, and Butler's *Analogy,* but, though expressing admiration for both, apparently found the grounds of their opposition to materialism unacceptable: at any rate, he had

[3] *Lectures on the English Poets, Works,* V, 167.
[4] *The Plain Speaker, Works,* VII, 226.
[5] *Lectures on the English Poets,* VIII, *Works,* V, 146.

already planned to write his own answer to one aspect of the materialist philosophy. He was also already specifically critical of associationism as an adequate theory of knowledge. All this appears from the essay "My First Acquaintance with Poets." [6] He says there: "I told Coleridge I had written a few remarks, and was sometimes foolish enough to believe that I had made a discovery on the same subject (the *Natural Disinterestedness of the Human Mind*)—and I tried to explain my view of it to Coleridge, who listened with great willingness, but I did not succeed in making myself understood." [7] A little later he says in describing his next meeting with Coleridge, "I broached to him an argument of mine to prove that *likeness* was not mere association of ideas. . . . He assented to the justness of this distinction . . . and John Chester listened; not from any interest in the subject, but because he was astonished that I should be able to suggest anything to Coleridge that he did not already know." [8]

[6] It is scarcely possible here to go into the point which Mr. Howe proves so thoroughly in his *Life of Hazlitt,* that Hazlitt's testimony regarding the facts of his own past is altogether reliable. Hazlitt had a remarkable memory for such things, and even the most violent of his prejudices never altered facts, though it might sometimes color them. One instance of the quality of his memory, which may be worth noting, occurs in connection with an inaccurate quotation from Wordsworth in the *Spirit of the Age* (1823). In the notes to the "White Doe of Rylstone" (1837) in which the lines were published for the first time, Wordsworth said that "this and the five lines that follow, were either read or recited by me, more than thirty years since, to the late Mr. Hazlitt, who quoted some expressions in them (imperfectly remembered) in a work of his published several years ago." (Howe, *Life,* p. 73 n.) No single reference or two can establish Hazlitt's accuracy to the facts of his life conclusively perhaps; but it would be impossible to read the *Life* through without being convinced of it.

[7] *Works,* XII, 266.

[8] *Ibid.,* p. 274. De Quincey in 1845 wrote that he had looked into Hazlitt's criticism of Hartley many years before, but had not liked the "tone" against Hartley, "and afterwards, hearing that Coleridge challenged for his own most of what was important in the thoughts," he "lost all interest in the essay." (De Quincey's *Works,* XI, 341 ff.) Such claims as this are by their

Hazlitt's philosophical direction, then, in the only important way in which it was similar to Coleridge's (in its opposition, that is, to the materialists) was already determined before he met the poet; in most other respects his philosophy was, from first to last, utterly un-Coleridgean, though there were two or three points, such as his early favorable but hazy impression of Kant, which he very likely received from Coleridge.

In literary matters the most conspicuous point of resemblance between the two critics is found in their Shakespearean criticism, and particularly in their accounts of the character of Hamlet. This is not strictly a part of our present subject; but since it bears somewhat upon general theory it may be summarized briefly. In the whole course of *The Characters of Shakespeare's Plays* Hazlitt does not once mention Coleridge, an omission which is not likely to have been accidental. On the other hand, his references to Schlegel are frequent. The year before the publication of this volume of criticism, Hazlitt had reviewed at length in the *Edinburgh Review* John Black's translation of Schlegel's *Lectures*.[9] And in preparing his own book he clearly had a copy of this translation before him. In the earlier portion of the volume there are frequent references

very nature impossible to disprove, but this one is at the very least highly improbable. Hazlitt was clearly more critical of associationism in the early days of his friendship with Coleridge than was the latter. Although by the time Hazlitt's essay was published in 1805 Coleridge had broken away from Hartley and might conceivably have furnished some arguments for Hazlitt, there was not at that time anything in the relations between the two to prevent Hazlitt's acknowledging such an obligation if it existed. The men were still friends, and Hazlitt's habit always was to make generous acknowledgment of the contributions of others. Moreover, it is impossible to escape the impression, from a reading of Coleridge's letters and published prose, that an idea which seemed to him good was almost always certain to sound to him like his own idea.—For the similarity of the views of Coleridge and Hazlitt on Hartley, see p. 31 ff., above.

9 In the number for February, 1816. Reprinted in Hazlitt's *Works*, X, 78 ff.

to and quotations from Schlegel, who is sometimes referred
to by name, sometimes as "an eminent critic." This occurs
very often throughout Hazlitt's criticism of Shakespeare's
tragedies, and here too there is often a close resemblance
between his interpretations and those of Schlegel. But
when he comes to the historical plays and later the
comedies [10] he ceases almost entirely to cite Schlegel's opinions and no longer moulds his own interpretations after
them. He seems thus to have gained in independence and
confidence as he warmed to the subject of his first sustained
work in criticism.[11]

One or two of the individual criticisms in this book of
Hazlitt's, notably the account of the character of Hamlet,
bears a closer resemblance to Coleridge's interpretation
than to Schlegel's, though all three are fundamentally alike.
It may be that in this case Hazlitt is borrowing Coleridge's
idea without acknowledgment. On the other hand it is
possible that both Coleridge and Hazlitt would have re-
acted against Schlegel's somewhat unsympathetic analysis
of the character while accepting its psychological truth—
and would thus have resembled each other independently.
No final conclusion regarding this relationship of Schlegel,
Coleridge, and Hazlitt is possible for several reasons. One
is that we have so little information about the content of
Coleridge's first two series of lectures dealing with Shake-

[10] This division is not exact: the *Tempest* and the *Midsummer Night's
Dream* are in the earlier part of the book and contain a good deal of
Schlegel.

[11] There is some interest, in view of Hazlitt's admiration of Schlegel, in
a passage from the Memoirs of Thomas Moore relating to a conversation
between himself and Schlegel: "Had much talk with Schlegel in the evening . . . spoke of Hazlitt, who, he said, l'avoit depasse in his critical
opinions, and was an ultra-Shakespearian."—Thomas Moore, *Memoirs,
Journal, and Correspondence*, ed. Lord John Russell. Entry of May, 1821,
III, 235.

speare—the first in 1808, the second in 1811–12. Neither do we know whether Hazlitt heard any of these lectures. He was in London during part at least of the time of both series. But during the 1808 series he was first ill and then preoccupied with the flurry of his impending marriage; and during the second he was in a state of anxiety and depression and very busy in preparation for his own set of lectures on philosophy which began before Coleridge's had ended. And Hazlitt's statement, already quoted, that he had never heard Coleridge or Wordsworth say much about Shakespeare, though he was obviously thinking of their conversation, would perhaps not have been made had he attended these lectures. Yet there is a little evidence that Hazlitt knew something of the content of one at least, that of December 16, 1811.[12] Coleridge himself would have settled the point finally, if one could depend upon the accuracy of his reminiscent statements, which one cannot do. For he claimed priority over Schlegel in the interpretation of Hamlet's character, and cited Hazlitt as witness to his having expressed it in conversation as early as the year 1798. But Coleridge's note on this was recorded many years later, and his faulty memory is well known. Hazlitt probably never saw this statement of Coleridge's, and might not have admitted its truth. A report in the *Champion* of one

[12] Evidence is based upon a remark cited by Hazlitt as that of "some critic" in his lecture on Shakespeare and Milton, which has been traced to Coleridge's lecture of that date (Howe's edition of Hazlitt, V, 388; 48 n). Hazlitt shows some familiarity with two of the later lectures which Coleridge delivered in 1818–19. His reference to the second of these is a passing one to an opinion uttered by Coleridge "in his late Lectures" in the *Letter to William Gifford* (Howe's edition, IX, 255). Upon an earlier lecture delivered at the beginning of February, 1818, Hazlitt wrote an entire essay for the *Yellow Dwarf* (Waller and Glover edition, XI, 416 ff.); and yet it is not clear that he had attended even this lecture, his references being largely to the report of it published in the *Courier* and to Coleridge's own prospectus for the course.

of Coleridge's Shakespearean lectures of 1818–19 says that Coleridge "at least accords with, if he has not availed himself of, the opinions of Hazlitt, and of another lecturer" on the character of Hamlet. The other lecturer was Thelwall, himself editor of the *Champion*. Mr. Raysor [13] characterizes the suggestion as "impudent" and obviously without foundation. Certainly Coleridge did not draw his ideas from Hazlitt as late as 1817 when *The Characters of Shakespeare's Plays* appeared. Mr. Raysor himself is convinced of Coleridge's independence, if not of his priority to Schlegel in this point.[14] There is, however, the possibility that the interpretation may have arisen in the course of conversation between Coleridge and Hazlitt and perhaps Lamb, in the early years of their acquaintance, and that Hazlitt may have contributed more than a pair of ears. For, after all, Coleridge was not above learning or taking suggestion from others,[15] and Hazlitt was for some years after their first meeting a person to whom Coleridge was willing to listen. There is no proof of Hazlitt's originality or even of his share in this, but the possibility should be mentioned. For Coleridge's louder claims and his greater fame both have caused students to assume rather more for him in certain respects than can be well substantiated.

Whatever may be the case with Hamlet, Coleridge's general influence upon Hazlitt consisted primarily in stimulating his interest in certain aspects of literature to which he had hitherto paid little attention. Coleridge was

[13] T. M. Raysor, *Coleridge's Shakespearean Criticism*. Mr. Raysor gives the best and most complete account of this whole question, with only incidental reference, however, to Hazlitt.—See I, li, lxi, 19; II, 323.

[14] He cites other evidence than Coleridge's own that Coleridge had given *some* interpretation of the character before the date of Schlegel's lectures.

[15] Cf. Hazlitt's remark that Lamb "has furnished many a text for C[oleridge] to preach upon." The *texts* were literary, not religious, as the passage shows.—Hazlitt, "On the Conversation of Authors," *Works*, VII, 36.

both a stimulus and a challenge to the younger man. What Hazlitt did in consequence was, not to follow him, but to chart for himself, very casually and in fragments, a course which was not, as we have already said, that of neo-Platonism, or of neo-classicism or sentimentalism, but which has most in common with eighteenth- (and indeed with twentieth-) century realism, with the acceptance of the world as it is—such as we find, say, in Fielding—but deepened under the influence of a more serious world, of a world which showed the face of more suffering and which demanded more sympathy than the old one.[16] Through the heights and depths of the French Revolution and the Napoleonic wars, and of the industrial revolution and its consequent economic changes, man is seen capable of rising —or sinking—to regions of experience undreamed by Augustan and earlier Georgian placidity. As in the Eliza-bethan period, life was rich enough during the young manhood of Hazlitt and Coleridge to furnish all elements of the tragic, the comic, or the ironic. In this lies a great difference between the early or "little romantic move-ment," as it has been called, of the eighteenth century, and the age with which we are concerned. It may be said that earlier eighteenth-century romanticism, insofar as it took the form of a literature of escape from reality, represented the escape from flatness and superficiality; whereas the writing of the greater romantic period, when it was an escape, represented for the most part escape from the tragic difficulties of life. The generation of Hazlitt and Coleridge

16 It would be possible to show that even Hazlitt's politics and political economy were not Utopian but realistic for the reason that they were not founded upon an idealization of human nature. A development of this point would not, however, come within the scope of the present subject.— See the essay on Bentham in the *Spirit of the Age,* and, in general, the *Polit-ical Essays,* the papers on Malthus, etc.

was like that of Shakespeare in that it had no need to go beyond the reality of this life because of a lack of sustenance for the imagination in the affairs of the times. But their age differed from Shakespeare's by reason of the more hopeful and adventurous if no less deeply moving character of the national life of Elizabeth's day. To accept life as it is, required therefore more courage (as far as a generalization of this kind is admissible) in the early nineteenth century than it had either in the eighteenth or at the end of the sixteenth; and the harmony which the greatest literature either finds or creates between fact and imagination was therefore more difficult to achieve. This idea provides no complete formula for the romantics: but it could perhaps be shown to have had its bearing upon the change to political conservatism of Wordsworth and Coleridge and upon the latter's later philosophical support of the doctrines of the Church of England "with a difference"; it sheds light upon Shelley's romanticism, and Scott's, and upon Lamb's remoteness; in the light of it Keats, as we know him from his later letters if not from his poetry, may be said to have been in his last years no longer a romantic at all—a development in him of which Hazlitt's full share can only be guessed.

The foregoing suggestion may sound rather like setting up realism as the only sane philosophy, and Hazlitt and the dying Keats as the only courageous philosophers of the age, but that is not intended. The objective validity of Platonic or realistic philosophies cannot be established: they still remain opposed as vehicles of thought for opposing temperaments. Each can be criticized destructively: to take the specific case, Hazlitt's realism may be partly the result of a deficient power of imagination; Coleridge's Platonism may represent in part merely a lack of courage.

This does not matter. But what does matter for the present purpose is to realize how deep was the division between them, and in what the division consisted.

The psychological subtlety of Coleridge's criticism is being more and more recognized. There is no question that in his power to describe many of the workings of the mind he is quite unmatched. His account of dramatic illusion as distinct from delusion [17] and his criticism of Wordsworth's poetry and poetic theory [18] are but two well-known instances out of many. What has not, however, been observed about Coleridge's criticism is that its power lies almost always in analysis of the *manner* and not the *motive* of thought. His introspective brilliance sheds much light upon the workings of a mind of genius and upon many universal modes of thought and feeling, but he had comparatively little insight into the fundamental springs of individual character and action.

It is in just this psychological province that Hazlitt's strength lay. One may take almost any of Hazlitt's accounts of his contemporaries in *The Spirit of the Age* as illustrations. Cobbett, he tells us, was one of those persons who are actuated by an inner necessity of fighting rather than by an inner conviction of truth. Such a statement as this goes to the root of character at once; it sets a dozen other qualities of Cobbett in their true light, at the same time that it marks vividly a recognizable type of human being. With this one might compare Coleridge's "Mr. Cobbett, who, for a dollar, can raise what, offer him ten thousand dollars, he could not allay." [19] Here is Coleridge characteristically pushing a man away from himself by a moral judgement

---

[17] Raysor, *op. cit.,* I, xxxviii ff. and 128 ff.
[18] *Biographia Literaria,* Chapters XVII–XXII.
[19] *Anima Poetae,* p. 216.

instead of trying to understand him. Hazlitt's view of Cobbett is historically more accurate; and it should be noted
that he had little more relish for Cobbett's politics than
had Coleridge.[20]

There is another aspect of Hazlitt's psychological insight
which is of a more general kind and yet is quite distinct
from that of Coleridge. Hazlitt remarks on one occasion
that "no one has ever yet seen through all the intricate
folds and delicate involutions of our self-love." [21] It is
true, no one has seen through them all; but Hazlitt saw
through a good many. He was introspective, and he was
willing to admit for himself as well as others that our
motives are not always what we think them. Sometimes
this carries him to the verge of cynicism, as when he ob-
serves with respect to a picture gallery: "We like subjects
of want, because they afford a relief to our own sense of
comfortlessness, and subjects of benevolence, because they
soothe our sense of self-importance—a feeling of which we
stand greatly in need." [22] On the other hand this insight
sometimes enables Hazlitt to anticipate in an almost star-
tling way some of the best and least questionable of modern
psychological views. In his essay on "Depth and Superficiality" he describes the effect of fear or disappointed affection. We may have a feeling that something is wrong,
he says, without even knowing what it is. In sleep we are

---

[20] The same kind of difference is observable at times in their Shakespearean criticism, but in this the similarities and contrasts are complicated
by the resemblance of each to Schlegel in so many points. The contrast
would, however, be fairly borne out by a careful comparison of the account
given by all three of the character of Iago.—See Hazlitt's *Works*, I, 206–
207; *Coleridge's Shakespearean Criticism*, I, 44–49; Schlegel's *Lectures*, pp.
402–403.—Hazlitt's superiority of insight into character becomes more pro-
nounced, however, in his later criticism.

[21] "On Depth and Superficiality," *Plain Speaker*, *Works*, VII, 352.

[22] *Notes of a Journey through France and Italy*, *Works*, IX, 125.

haunted by distress or desired bliss. The fear of looking our situation in the face gives the mind a "wandering and un-settled turn, makes our waking thoughts a troubled dream, or sometimes ends in madness, without any violent parox-ysm, without any severe pang, without any *overt act,* but from that silent operation of the mind which preys inter-nally upon itself, and works the decay of its powers the more fatally, because we dare not give it open and avowed scope." There is health of mind as well as of body, and when this is deranged we may feel pain or discomfort though the cause has been removed. "Our unconscious im-pressions necessarily give a colour to, and re-act upon our conscious ones; and it is only when these two sets of feeling are in accord, that our pleasures are true and sincere; where there is a discordance and misunderstanding in this re-spect, they are said (not absurdly as is pretended) to be false and hollow." [23]

In all this Hazlitt's difference from Coleridge is clearly marked. He has not the range nor the power of abstrac-tion, nor in some respects the intellectual subtlety of Coleridge. On the other hand, this kind of insight, which is one of Hazlitt's most striking powers, was to Coleridge, from the unrecognized conflicts of his own character, an almost closed door. For Coleridge was never able to "ac-cept" himself, as the psychologists say, on a natural plane: he had, that is, always to justify his actions, always to see himself reflected in others' eyes (and in his own too) with admiration. He must be a great moral leader, a great and

[23] *Plain Speaker, Works,* VII, 353–354.—One might note also such re-marks as that "those who are at war with others are not at peace with them-selves" ("Lady Morgan's Life of Salvator," *Works,* X, 280); or that we only sneer at others because we feel a lack of something in ourselves (*Works,* IX, 93).—See also the article "Manners Make the Man" in *New Writings, Second Series,* p. 152.

magnanimous friend, a philosopher who has for the first
time "entirely extricated the notions of time and space."
His own genuine greatness was not enough, he must be
hardly less than perfect. And if he cannot be quite perfect,
the responsibility for any blemish must be placed outside
himself.[24] The chapter of his own deepest motives and conflicts was one which he could not endure to open; it therefore remained very nearly closed to him in the lives of
others.

Hazlitt and Coleridge, then, as critics worked to some
degree in different spheres; nor was the distinction merely
that the latter attempted to lay down canons which the
former either applied to specific writings or ignored in his
outbursts of enthusiasm. There is the further fact that
Coleridge's sphere was largely that of the mind, Hazlitt's
that of the emotions; or, more accurately, that Coleridge
dealt primarily with the mind and its relation to such
general emotions of mankind as do not find expression in
individual action, Hazlitt with emotion especially in its
relation to character and action. There is a paradox here
in the fact that Coleridge's subject matter seems more
purely æsthetic than Hazlitt's; while his attitude toward it,

[24] Coleridge's anguish over his use of opium will immediately come to
mind. We cannot say, of course, that Coleridge never admitted himself
wrong in anything. The statement is only relative, marking a general
tendency—for he had occasional moments of self-revelation. Even in regard
to the taking of opium, however, he rather insistently attributed his original
use of the drug to ill health; and he traced his ill health to an episode of
his childhood in which no responsibility attached to himself. The fact
that this may have been quite true is irrelevant, since the significance lies
in the urgency with which he justified himself. The truth was that Coleridge
could not tolerate the idea which, at bottom, he actually had of himself;
and that his life was spent in trying to escape from his own image. For a
development of something like this view of Coleridge's character the reader
is referred to an excellent article in the [London] *Times Literary Supplement*, No. 1,589 (July 14, 1932). This article represents very closely the
view of the present writer.

especially in his later years, is less disinterested, more moralistic, and consequently less purely æsthetic than Hazlitt's attitude toward his own subjects.

Theory of Imagination

Hazlitt appears to have had comparatively little interest in some of the questions that engrossed Coleridge and Wordsworth. This is notably true of the theory of imagination, even though on this he had in the end a good deal to say. For the term imagination Hazlitt is apt to invent and insert parenthetically a new definition whenever he has occasion to use the word. In writing of the drama of Racine he remarks that the French are a people devoid of "the faculty of imagination, if by this we mean the power of placing things in the most novel and striking point of view." [25] But we do not generally mean that, and neither does Hazlitt, although this definition finds some parallel in the writing of Coleridge, and, still more, of Wordsworth, where the function of the poet is sometimes said to be just that of placing old things in a new light. Again, imagination is the finding of similarity in things which are essentially similar, as contrasted with wit, which consists in finding similarities in things generally unlike.[26] And, in an erratic moment in the essay on "Will-Making," he speaks of "that innate love of inequality and injustice, which is the favourite principle of the imagination." [27]

On the other hand, he has more serious moments than these; and his earliest account of the faculty borrows interest from the fact that it precedes by some years the earliest published remarks on the subject by Wordsworth

[25] *Notes of a Journey Through France and Italy, Works,* IX, 115–116.
[26] "On Wit and Humour," *Lectures on the English Comic Writers, Works,* VIII, 23.
[27] *Table-Talk, Works,* VI, 115.

and Coleridge. The passage,[28] written in or before 1805, approaches the question from the philosophical and not the literary angle. Imagination, he says, is the "faculty of multiplying, varying, extending, combining, and comparing" our original "passive impressions." The materials from which it is composed are those of memory. It is the power by which we combine impressions leading toward action; *it is necessary to all action and all knowledge.* In regard to the future, toward which all action is necessarily directed, man "creates the object, he pushes his ideas beyond the bounds of his memory and senses." It is in the nature of the imagination to alter the order in which things have been impressed on the senses and even "to modify these impressions in a very great degree." He calls this faculty sometimes a "reasoning imagination."

There are several interesting things about this passage. One is, as has been said, its date in anticipating publication of the later poetic doctrine of the faculty as an "endowing or modifying power" which also "shapes and creates." [29] There is interest too in the fact of its resemblance to the view of Kant, who likewise considered the imagination as an essential element in the acquisition of knowledge and a universal faculty of mankind. And Hazlitt was using it for the same purpose, that of undermining the empiricist philosophy. Hazlitt, however, is probably indebted for the idea to Coleridge, who as early as 1802 had written in a letter to Sotheby [30] of "fancy or the aggregating faculty of the mind" as contrasted with "imagination, or the modifying and coadunating faculty." Coleridge had originally conceived of the imagination not as a universal possession

[28] *Essay on the Principles of Human Action, Works,* VII, 404 ff.
[29] Wordsworth, Preface to the 1815 edition of his poems.
[30] *Letters,* I, 405.

of man, but as a rare gift possessed by few. Only after the
year 1801, when he seems to have begun his serious study
of Kant, did he come to a broader interpretation of the
term which culminated in the theory summarized at the
end of the thirteenth chapter of the *Biographia Literaria*,
of the imagination as either primary or secondary, the
former being the "living Power and prime Agent of all
human Perception," and "a repetition in the finite mind of
the eternal act of creation in the infinite I AM." [31]

It should be observed that if Hazlitt's passage does reflect the influence of Coleridge's conversation, his view is
nearer to Kant than to Coleridge, for he stops short with
imagination as the active power of the mind in acquiring
knowledge without supposing that it gives to man's knowledge an objective validity beyond human sensuous experience, or that it enables man to apprehend the Deity or
universal reality.[32] Thus, Hazlitt's scepticism was with him
apparently from the beginning, as Coleridge's fundamentally Platonic temperament was with him. Even had
there been no political differences between them it is
doubtful whether Hazlitt's admiration for Coleridge or
their mutual respect would have continued very long to
bridge that gap.

The importance of this conception of the imagination
for Hazlitt's philosophy is obvious, for it furnishes the
keystone of his criticism of the sensationalists' and the associationists' theory of the mind. He identifies the imagination with that "active principle" which distinguishes the

[31] For the history of Coleridge's development of this idea see the Introduction (p. xxxiii ff.) to Shawcross's edition of the *Biographia Literaria*,
to which I am indebted for much that appears in this passage.

[32] This again makes one wonder what might have been the effect upon
Hazlitt's philosophy had he come to know Kant through other than Platonic interpreters.

human mind, in his opinion, from Locke's *tabula rasa:*
"the mind alone is formative," he says, and that formative
faculty is imagination. Yet, important as this link is in his
philosophy, he seems to have dropped it entirely, for it
does not recur in any of his later work.[33]

His only other serious account of the imagination is a
brief definition in the first of the *Lectures on the English
Poets.* He has evidently just been reading Wordsworth's
Preface of 1815 and the *Essay Supplementary to the Preface,* which very likely suggested, or at least influenced, his
definition of imagination as "that faculty which represents
objects, not as they are in themselves, but as they are
moulded by other thoughts and feelings, into an infinite
variety of shapes and combinations of power." The language of imagination is "not the less true to nature, because
it is false in point of fact; but so much the more true and
natural, if it conveys the impression which the object
under the influence of passion makes on the mind." [34] On
another occasion, in speaking of what he considers the lack
of imagination in French art, he defines the imaginative
power as that of "giving the feeling that there is in
nature." [35]

[33] The fact of his having dropped this idea perhaps strengthens the
probability that he had received it from someone else, most likely Coleridge
—and had failed to make it a part of his own habitual thought. For all the
many occasions on which he speaks of the "active principle in the mind"
he only once takes this step of identifying it with imagination.

[34] "On Poetry in General," *Works,* V, 4. Wordsworth says in the *Essay
Supplementary to the Preface* of 1815, that the poet must treat of things
"not as they *are,* but as they *appear;* not as they exist in themselves, but as
they *seem* to exist to the *senses* and to the *passions.*" Coleridge's view is
similar.

[35] *Notes of a Journey Through France and Italy, Works,* IX, 128. There
is a confusion in the expression and perhaps also in the thought of "the
feeling that there is in nature," which is not altogether clarified by recognition of the fact that Hazlitt is here probably referring primarily to human
nature.

Interestingly enough, though in his earliest account of the imaginative faculty Hazlitt, as we have seen, employed, probably under the influence of Coleridge, the term "reasoning imagination," yet in his review of the *Biographia Literaria* he refuses to discuss Coleridge's distinction between *imagination* and *fancy*,[36] and says only, respecting the former, that "reason and imagination are both excellent things; but perhaps their provinces ought to be kept more distinct than they have lately been." [37] And some years later in *The Plain Speaker* he published an essay "On Reason and Imagination" [38] in which the two terms, though not formally discussed for the purpose of definition, are used to represent antithetical tendencies of the mind. Reason as seeking truth by formulas, generalizations, and maps is contrasted much to its disadvantage with imagination, which sees the individual object and takes into account the imponderables of passion and sympathy. The whole paper, however, has the air of being an "occasional" essay, inspired by some instance of narrow logic (called *reason* here) which he does not specifically

[36] Hazlitt continues to use these terms interchangeably in the manner common to that time, and appears to have had no interest in the endeavors of both Coleridge and Wordsworth to distinguish them. In one passage, however, which may have been written by Hazlitt, Coleridge's distinction is assumed. This occurs in an article on "Moore and Byron" from the *Edinburgh Review*, published as Hazlitt's by Mr. Howe in the appendix to Vol. XVI of the *Complete Works*. In his discussion of a number of these articles written for Jeffrey Mr. Howe points out certain passages which he considers to be the editor's own, and discards two entire articles which Messrs. Waller and Glover had included, as being not primarily by Hazlitt. I find it impossible not to question the attribution to Hazlitt of the first part, at least down to the middle of page 413, of this newly included article on Moore and Byron, though there is no doubt that he wrote the final portion. The passage relating to imagination and fancy, on page 414, may be Hazlitt's: at least it runs continuously in thought with a following section which is undoubtedly his (see Howe's edition, XVI, 413 ff.).

[37] "Coleridge's Literary Life," *Works*, X, 157.

[38] *Works*, VII, 44 ff.

mention. He does, however, still speak of the imagination as an *associating* principle, and one which has "an instinctive perception when a thing belongs to a system, or is only an exception to it."

In spite of all this variety and even eccentricity in Hazlitt's uses and definitions of the term, a fairly consistent notion of the faculty of imagination does arise. It is that of a power essential for all human knowledge, the forward projection of thought arising from a new *combination* of impressions such as occurs when the scientist makes a new discovery or projects a new theory, as well as when the common man learns something that is new to himself. But since both thought and feeling are involved in any act of the human mind, the exercise of this power is not confined to external facts, but is exerted upon the feelings of men as well; and here lies the peculiar province of the poet. Only, in neither case is the apparent access of knowledge or understanding to be looked upon as more than a *feeling of understanding,* or as more than a knowledge valid within the inescapable limits of man's nature. It is never a knowledge of transcendent reality, as it is with Coleridge.

The interrelation of Coleridge, Wordsworth, and Hazlitt on the subject is emphasized by the fact that all three choose for illustration of the use of this faculty in literature passages from the great scenes of Lear on the heath. Wordsworth dilates upon the imaginative use of the word *hang* in the lines about "one who gathers samphire" on the cliff.[39] Hazlitt in the first lecture on the English poets already referred to, cites Lear's apostrophe to the heavens "for they are old like him." [40] And Coleridge cites, "What!

[39] Preface to the second edition of the *Lyrical Ballads.*
[40] *Works,* V, 4.

have his daughters brought him to this pass!" and the "preceding apostrophe to the elements." [41]

Painting and Poetry

On the whole, Hazlitt was less interested in the specifically æsthetic problems of literature than in those of painting. This was no doubt in part because the deliberate revolt against formalism and convention in poetry was already, with Wordsworth and Coleridge, in such good hands—which was not the case with the art of painting. There was another more personal reason as well. The two arts had each meant something quite different to Hazlitt as a vocation. Upon painting the loftiest ambitions of his youth had been set. Dreams of his own greatness would haunt him as he wandered through a picture gallery. He could imagine himself now and then as being able to paint like Rembrandt. His fond lingering memory in later days of his early attempts at painting is evidence of how far this art had been the vehicle for his own desire for achievement. Some of the same feeling he had with regard to philosophy and his early *Essay on the Principles of Human Action*. But he seems to have had none of that feeling for literature. There he is purely the disinterested critic or analyst—never (or very rarely, in a few passages on prose style) the fellow-artist. This is not to say that his later success as a periodical writer gave him no satisfaction. He liked, as he tells us, to be pointed out on the "fives court" as a writer in the *Edinburgh Review*. It gave him a certain self-esteem; it gave him an adequate place in the eyes of the world; and it helped to rub away some of the soreness left by political attacks upon him and

[41] *Biographia Literaria*, Chapter IV.

perhaps also by his domestic infelicities. But it did not
fire those dreams of admiration in the eyes of remote pos-
terity, that passion for immortal fame which he in common
with his age—in common, indeed, with all ages until very
recently—believed to be itself one of the noblest of passions. Hence with Hazlitt the reading of books tended to
be in one sense a more passive enjoyment than his perusal
of pictures, and he is more often content to tell us simply
how he feels about them with little active desire to tell us
how we should write them.

Yet, aside from his own ambitions, literature was to
him at least as important as painting—indeed it often
seems to him superior. At the very end of his life, in the
essay on "The Sick Chamber" he says that books let us
into the souls of others and lay open to us the secret of
our own: "they are the first and last, the most home-felt,
the most heart-felt of all our enjoyments." [42]

In his familiar essays Hazlitt often associates painting
with poetry, if rather casually. "Books, pictures, and the
face of·nature" sometimes seem to him the most permanent of all human enjoyments. But in his criticism proper
he seldom dwells upon the unity of all the arts and their
common purpose. "As to what your correspondent adds
of painting and poetry being the same thing," he remarks
on one occasion,[43] "it is an old story which I do not believe." Nor does he attempt any ordered classification of
all the arts in respect to their difference in purpose or medium. But he often contrasts those two which to him were
greatest, painting and poetry. Though not in an antithetical, at least in a relative sense he distinguished them as
objective and subjective. Painting "reveals the face of

[42] *Works*, XII, 130.
[43] *Works*, IX, 483.

nature"; while poetry, the language of feeling, of passion
and imagination, "paints the heart of man." [44] The latter
constitutes, in a sense, an embodiment, the other a disem-
bodiment. This distinction works out favorably sometimes
to one of the arts, sometimes to the other. In discussing
Lear Hazlitt finds himself convinced that "the language
of poetry is superior to the language of painting; because
the strongest of our recollections relate to feelings, not to
faces." [45] On the other hand in "The Pleasures of Painting" [46] he sees the matter in the contrary light, for he
finds the experience of painting satisfying and that of
writing not so. In one you "translate feelings into words,"
in the other "names into things." Painting is "a continual
creation out of nothing": in it "the form of beauty is
changed into a substance: the dream and the glory of the
universe is made 'palpable to feeling as to sight' . . . like
a bubble reflecting the mighty fabric of the universe."
Wordsworth's poetical phrase Hazlitt here borrows to describe the painter, who understands "the texture and
meaning of the visible universe, and 'sees into the life of
things.' "

Often, when nothing forcibly directs his attention to
the subject of poetry as a whole, Hazlitt tends to associate
its name with only those limited kinds of poetry which
belonged to the eighteenth century, and which were still
the most fashionable productions of the early nineteenth.
At these times he saw poetry as the voice of artifice, of
triviality, or of escape from reality, while painting was by
contrast the expression of truth: "Even where there is
neither beauty nor use—if that ever were—still there is

[44] *Lectures on the English Poets, Works,* V, 1; and "On People of Sense,"
Plain Speaker, Works, VII, 245; also IX, 129.
[45] "Lear," *Characters of Shakespeare's Plays, Works,* I, 271.
[46] *Table-Talk, Works,* VI, 5 ff.

truth," he says of the painter's subjects.[47] This he conceives as the truth of external phenomena, modified always by the painter's own feeling, but not, like poetry,
created almost entirely out of that feeling alone. Poets
if they do not find things delightful make them so. They
"feign the beautiful and grand out of their own minds,
and imagine all things to be, not what they are, but what
they ought to be. They are naturally inventors, creators
of truth, of love, and beauty." Insofar as they are this they
are both delightful and admirable.[48] But there is nothing
in the medium of poetry, in words, which are themselves
mere symbols, to compel the poet to keep "his eye on the
object." Hence there is no check upon his passion or prejudice. When he writes of the moods of his own mind he
needs no check; but when he deals with external facts he
is in danger of doing great harm. His "invention" then
may become false to the more universal truth.[49]

Whether it is possible or not to consider either poetry
or painting as the greatest of the arts, it is possible, Hazlitt feels, to mark out certain limitations of each in respect
to the other. The peculiar province of each is to give that
which cannot so well be given by the other. "That picture
is of little comparative value which can be completely
translated into another language,—of which the description in a common catalogue conveys all that is expressed
by the picture itself: for it is the excellence of every art
to give what can be given by no other, in the same degree." It is a sign of the failure of the English school in
"heroic or classical" painting, that not one painter has

[47] *Ibid.,* p. 10.
[48] "On Poetical Versatility," *Round Table, Works,* I, 151–152.
[49] This idea, it is needless to say, is inspired by Wordsworth's and Southey's patriotic poetry and other writing of the kind, in which Hazlitt feels that party prejudice is masquerading as universal truth.

succeeded in making as great an impression by visible means as has been excited by the same subject through the medium of words.[50]

In an article on American literature published in 1829 Hazlitt takes up this subject from a slightly different angle. Here he seems to approach Lessing's idea of temporal and spatial continuity as a distinguishing limit of the two arts.[51] He complains of the endless details in the novels of Fenimore Cooper which halt the progress of the story. Cooper, he says, seems unaware that an "abridgment" is all that is either possible or desirable in even the most individual representation in literature. Cooper describes an Indian chief to his very buttonholes. This is to mistake the province of the writer for that of the artist: "it is this very obligation of painting and statuary to fill up all the details, that renders them incapable of telling a story, or of expressing more than a single moment, group, or figure." [52] Poetry and fiction do not deal in these particulars but make up for their lack of completeness "by a more rapid march and an intuitive glance at the more striking results." Cooper "runs riot in an account of the dishes at a boarding-house, as if it were a banquet of the Gods." [53] Hazlitt's objection to this kind of "high finish-

---

[50] "Fine Arts," *Works*, IX, 406–407.

[51] It is fairly certain, however, that Hazlitt had not read Lessing and knew his theories, if at all, only by hearsay. Hazlitt's view is actually little beyond that which Dryden indicates in his comparison between painting and tragedy in the *Essay* prefixed to his translation of Du Fresnoy's *Art of Painting*. Diderot also anticipated certain of Lessing's ideas in saying that the different arts must do different things. He advises the poet to give but one or two traits rather than a complete description.—Morley, *op. cit.*, II, 81–82.—If Hazlitt required a source for this idea, perhaps Diderot is the most probable one.

[52] Cf. the statement that "painting gives the event, poetry the progress of events" in the first of his *Lectures on the English Poets*, *Works*, V, 10.

[53] "American Literature—Dr. Channing," *Works*, X, 312–313.

ing" of detail (he applies to it the painter's term) implies
thus a limitation of the. proper province of literature—
and incidentally a protest as well against a certain kind of
"realism" which was just beginning to appear.

Painting, on the other hand, is, or should be, subject to
another limitation besides that of representing only a moment in time. It should represent, Hazlitt says, "the visible, not the invisible." Allegory and symbolism are not
its proper province.[54] Benjamin West's much-heralded picture of "Death on the Pale Horse" is here under criticism.
The attributes of Death are infinitely wide and general;
it is a mighty abstraction "like Night, or Space, or Time."
The impression which it makes is essentially visionary: its
reality is in "the mind's eye" alone, and therefore the least
definite medium of expression is the best; no physical
form can really represent the idea, though it may be suggested by the more "unformed and insubstantial," the "less
bodily" presence of words. Thus Chaucer's story of the
three rioters, through the very vagueness of its symbolism,
can suggest what West's picture fails to represent.[55]

Poetry

With the provinces of painting and poetry distinguished as portraying, the one, the face of nature, the
other the mind of man, Hazlitt's opinion of the dignity

[54] Cf. Winckelmann's contrary opinion, that the painter should attempt
allegory, and that the "most eminent prerogative" of painting is "the representation of invisible, past and future things."—*Reflections on the Painting and Sculpture of the Greeks*, by Winckelmann, translated into English
in 1765 by Fuseli. It is very likely, though not certain, that Hazlitt knew
this work.

[55] "West's Picture of Death on the Pale Horse," *Works*, IX, 321; *Lectures
on the English Poets, Works*, V, 33-34.—There is one painting, however,
which Hazlitt feels to be an exception to this rule. Rembrandt's "Jacob's
Dream" does give precisely that grand and insubstantial, visionary effect.
This was a picture which Hazlitt never tired of praising; to him it was a

of poetry varied from time to time along with his opinion
of the dignity of the human mind in relation to nature.
Often his moods of disillusion dominate. Man is then a
poor thing as compared with the "universal face of nature," and the poet sinks with the rest of mankind until
his work is no more than "glittering tinsel" and airy
nothings.

In his treatment of lyric poetry Hazlitt appears to share
the current assumption, inherited from the seventeenth
and eighteenth centuries, that the lyric is to be regarded,
however beautiful in individual instances it may be, as a
minor form, almost a by-product of the poet's art, whose
real business is with the larger forms. Lyric poetry, he remarks in the *Lectures on the English Poets,* is more like
painting than any other sort of poetry; "it deals in hier-
oglyphics and passing figures, which depend for effect, not
on the working out, but on the selection. It is the dance
and pantomime of poetry." [56] It may, however, be partly
the more specific influence of Bacon, who was a pervading
presence in Hazlitt's thought on many subjects, that limited Hazlitt's conception of lyric poetry at times. In a
passage of the *Advancement of Learning* from which
Hazlitt had already quoted in his first lecture Bacon divides poetry into "Poesie Narrative, Representative, and
Allusive"; that is, into narrative, dramatic, and (as he explains the last term) allegorical or "parabolical." [57] He
thus has no place for the lyric.

This theoretical neglect of lyric poetry had long been
quite customary; but Wordsworth's now famous definition
of poetry as the *spontaneous overflow of powerful feelings*

perpetual, and an inexplicable, marvel.—See *Works,* IX, 21, and often elsewhere.
  [56] Lecture IV, *Works,* V, 81.
  [57] Book III, Chapter 13.

is of a kind to suggest that he was thinking of lyric rather,
at least, than narrative or dramatic poetry; and from his
time on the lyric gradually established its claims in criticism. Hazlitt's philosophy, however, would tend to rein-
force the older view: one who recognized a moral obligation to transcend as far as possible his own individual
experience and enter into that of others, who held this
rather than the ideal of self-evolution or self-fulfillment
as the goal for individual striving—such a person would
perhaps naturally incline to understand greatness better
in drama than in lyrical forms. Partly at least for this reason Hazlitt, though he wrote much fine criticism of poetry
and often appraised it justly, sometimes seems to belittle
the poet's art and often appears satisfied with the notion
of poetry (of non-dramatic poetry) as a decorative art, and
of the poet as an irresponsible pursuer of casual and unrelated "beauties." In his essay "On the Spirit of Monarchy" he remarks that man is "a poetical animal and
delights in fiction" because he likes to have scope for the
exercise of "mere will." We need only the merest "peg or
loop to hang our idle fancies on" and rejoice in the sense
of power we get from making kings of mere men and
Gods of sticks and stones.[58] In such passages as this, poetry
is conceived of as creative, but not as very closely related
to the "nobler" feelings of man.

This drawing-room conception of poetry appears, however, only when Hazlitt's attention is centered upon something else. When he directs his mind seriously and exclusively to poetry, what he says is rather different. His fullest
discussion of the subject is in the first of the *Lectures on
the English Poets,* that "On Poetry in General." In preparing this introductory lecture Hazlitt seems to have

[58] *Works,* XII, 242.

turned to the criticism prefixed and appended to Wordsworth's poems, for the essay contains a number of phrases
and allusions which recall this. He has also been re-
reading or is recalling the remarks on poetry in Bacon's
Advancement of Learning, to which he refers by name.
Saintsbury in his *History of Criticism,*[59] writing of this
first lecture, says that much of it is "directly Coleridgean,"
without, however, attempting to analyze the thought of
either Coleridge or Hazlitt on the subject of poetry. Actually there appears to be little "direct" resemblance beyond
the generally romantic emphasis upon feeling, imagination, and spontaneity. The main thread of the lecture and
the ideas as a whole suggest that Wordsworth's, and probably also Coleridge's, theories acted upon him as a stimulus, rather than a source, for the formulation of his own.
The lecture opens with the definition of poetry as "the
natural impression of any object or event, by its vividness
exciting an involuntary movement of imagination and
passion, and producing, by sympathy, a certain modulation
of the voice, or sounds, expressing it." It is "the language of
the imagination and the passions"; for whenever a sense
of beauty, or power, or harmony, is felt, there is poetry,
"in its birth." [60] Hazlitt believes, in an even more unre-
served sense than does Wordsworth, that any feeling which
is genuine and in any degree communicable, or any object
or event which arouses spontaneous feeling, is a fit subject
for poetry: "the shepherd-boy is a poet, when he first
crowns his mistress with a garland of flowers; . . . the city-
apprentice, when he gazes after the Lord-Mayor's show;
the miser, when he hugs his gold." [61]

[59] III, 254.
[60] "On Poetry in General," *Works,* V, 1.
[61] *Ibid.,* p. 2.

But poetry is no mere diversion. It has rightly been called a "graver" study than history; for its materials lie deeper within man's nature. Feeling is more fundamental than pure intellect. Poetry is not—and here Hazlitt reverses what in less thoughtful moods he has written elsewhere—an escape from reality, a mere fiction created out of our wishes.[62] Like painting, poetry is an imitation of nature, even when it seems to represent not *what is* but *what we desire,* since the imagination and passions of man are themselves a part of nature. Poetry is not the less true to nature because it is false to fact, but rather the more true "if it conveys the impression which the object under the influence of passion makes on the mind." [63] Of these two kinds of truth, marked off by Hazlitt for the moment as *truth to fact* and *truth to nature*—the truth, that is, of science as against that of poetry—the latter is ill exchanged for the former: "let the naturalist, if he will, catch the glowworm, carry it home with him in a box, and find it next morning nothing but a little gray worm; let the poet . . . visit it at evening, when beneath the scented hawthorn and the crescent moon, it has built itself a palace of emerald light. This is also one part of nature, one appearance which the glowworm presents, and that not the least interesting; so poetry is one part of the history of the human mind, though it is neither science nor philosophy." [64]

This brings Hazlitt to a consideration of a topic also treated by Wordsworth, that of the relation between science and poetry, and the question whether the advance of the former is destructive of the latter. Wordsworth has

[62] Or if it is this, he says, at least "there is no other nor better reality."—*Ibid.,* p. 3.
[63] *Ibid.,* pp. 4, 8.
[64] *Ibid.,* p. 9.

said that poetry is "the breath and finer spirit of all knowledge," and that the poet will follow always in the steps of
science and will use its remotest discoveries as his proper
material "if the time should ever come when these things
shall be familiar to us, and the relations under which they
are contemplated . . . shall be manifestly and palpably
material to us as enjoying and suffering beings." [65] Hazlitt
maintains a different opinion. He thinks that the progress
of scientific knowledge has a tendency to circumscribe the
imagination, whose province is "principally visionary, the
unknown and undefined." Both "religious and poetical
enthusiasm" have received a shock from the modern ex-
perimental science and philosophy and from the comparative security of more civilized life: there can never be
another Jacob's Dream, for "the heavens have gone farther off, and grown astronomical." [66] This view of Hazlitt's is not in entire accord with his favorite remark that
poetry "comes home to the bosoms and businesses of men,"
a quotation from Bacon which fits Wordsworth's theory
better than his own at this point.

On the subject of poetry, then, Hazlitt swings alter-
nately between the conception of it as *escape* and the
conception of it as *knowledge* or *truth*. The integration
of the two ideas he seems constantly on the point of
achieving, but never quite does—never, at least, becomes
clearly aware that he is reconciling them. The key to their
reconciliation lies in the fact that what we escape from,
in the "poetry of escape" is the pressure of our own inade-
quacy, of our cosmic ignorance, the inevitable incompleteness of all human knowledge and experience. Poetry may
rescue us momentarily from this incompleteness, may give

[65] Preface to the second edition of the *Lyrical Ballads*.
[66] "On Poetry in General," *Works*, V, 9.

us an illusion of truth, a "feeling of knowledge" by creating a world of its own in the realms of imagination, where our knowledge may seem to be complete and not subject to the tests of science or of external experience. Or poetry may in another way allay our sense of incompleteness while leaving us in our own world, by an actual increase, through the poet's insight, of the sum of our knowledge of human life. In either case this *knowledge* is to be thought of as an emotion rather than an intellectual apprehension—it is the *identification* of subject and object, of the knower and the thing known; and the feeling remains the same whether the knowledge (or the object of knowledge) be considered as having objective reality or as being no more than a mode of thought inherent in the constitution of the mind. It is the mood "in which," as Wordsworth recognized it,

> The burthen of the mystery,
> In which the heavy and the weary weight
> Of all this unintelligible world,
> Is lightened:—

while "we see into the life of things" [67]—or think that we do. It is, as Hazlitt sees it, the source of the pleasure we take even in tragic poetry because it "gives an obvious relief to the indistinct and importunate cravings of the will . . . For knowledge is conscious power," and the mind no longer feels itself the dupe even though it may be the victim of vice or folly.[68] Hazlitt, then, recognizes this power in the arts, but he never brings it into complete focus with his two otherwise opposed conceptions of poetry.

[67] *Tintern Abbey.* Wordsworth is here speaking of nature, not poetry, but the experience described is essentially the æsthetic experience in general.

[68] "On Poetry in General," *Works,* V, 8.

In his statement, just quoted, that "knowledge is conscious power," we have a reference to a psychological truth which Hazlitt perhaps more clearly than any of his contemporaries realized. To De Quincey we owe the distinction between the "literature of knowledge" and the "literature of power"; and in general the full recognition of the connection of the sense of power with the æsthetic sense has been by students of criticism attributed to him. Miss A. E. Powell in *The Romantic Theory of Poetry* states that both Wordsworth and Coleridge "were conscious, in their intercourse with Nature, of the communication of power" and that Coleridge and De Quincey both recognized this communication of power as the mark of genius; [69] De Quincey's further development of the notion of "power" as contrasted with "knowledge" in literature she discusses also in another passage.[70] But long before De Quincey's idea was developed Hazlitt had habitually regarded the sense of power as a dominant characteristic of the human mind, had constantly called attention to the necessity of recognizing power and the desire for power as a psychological motive for action. He also saw perhaps more clearly than others—at least he emphasized more consistently—the relation between the sense of power and the æsthetic sense.[71] In the lecture on "Poetry in General" it will be remembered, Hazlitt said that "wherever a sense of beauty, or power, or harmony" exists, there is poetry "in its birth." The sense of power, he says in a later passage, "is as strong a principle in the mind as the love of pleasure"; and this sense it is that the poet gratifies by an

69 Chapter V, p. 145.
70 Chapter VI, p. 171 ff.
71 See especially the passage quoted on p. 45, above, in which Hazlitt clearly draws the distinction between science and art: "the one is knowledge—the other power." This passage was published in January, 1814.

extreme or complete expression of any of the feelings or passions of mankind. Indeed the mere expression of emotion in itself constitutes power; and the power is shared by the reader of the poet's work, for in reading he re-expresses or re-creates the feeling for himself.[72] But again this sense of power comes only when the expression carries with it something new—gives an added knowledge (or seeming knowledge), a new view of nature or man—and thus satisfies that "craving of the will," lightens the "burthen of the mystery"; the power is in the sense of an enlarged scope of feeling or activity.[73]

Poetry may be said to constitute a "literature of power" in the degree to which it springs from the creative imagination. For, though the materials of poetry are to be found in nature, a mere transcript of them does not make poetry. On this point Hazlitt quotes Bacon: poetry "has something divine in it, because it raises the mind and hurries it into sublimity, by conforming the shows of things to the desires of the soul, instead of subjecting the soul to external things, as reason and history do." [74] It is

[72] "On Poetry in General," *Works*, V, 7 ff. Cf. also *Works*, I, 176, 214; VII, 9; XII, 242.

[73] It seems most likely that De Quincey was indebted to Hazlitt for something of his view of "power" in literature. His ideas are very similar except as they refer to the philosophical idealism which he shared with Coleridge, and it is noteworthy that in explaining this idea he uses Hazlitt's favorite illustration of Jacob's Ladder. In the matter of priority of publication there can be no doubt. Hazlitt had clearly enunciated the idea as early as 1814; De Quincey explained his ideas in the *Letters to a Young Man whose Education has been neglected*, in 1823; and in the *Essay on Pope*, 1848. It is certain that on another occasion he borrowed from Hazlitt's writing without acknowledgment. (For an account of this, with the controversy between the two over their criticism of Malthus, see Howe's *Life*, pp. 364–365.) It might be shown from other points also that by De Quincey as well as others Hazlitt was "more read than praised, more imitated than extolled," as an anonymous reviewer in 1837 put it.

[74] Bacon's actual words are: "And therefore it [poetry] was ever thought to have some participation of divineness, because it doth raise and erect the

the creative imagination that moulds the materials of poetry into "an infinite variety of shapes and combinations of power." By its force is created "impassioned poetry," which is "an emanation of the moral and intellectual part of our nature, as well as of the sensitive—of the desire to know, the will to act, and the power to feel," and which, in order to be perfect, ought to appeal to all these aspects of our constitution.

Holding such views as these, Hazlitt was naturally opposed on theory to didactic poetry. He criticizes—of all people—Lord Byron for speaking of moral and didactic poetry as the highest class of that art. Because such things as morality are good in themselves, he inquires, "does it follow that they are the better for being put into rhyme?" [75] He professes to hate disputes in poetry even more than in religion, for he considers that "whatever appeals to the imagination, ought to rest on undivided sentiment, on one undisputed tradition, one catholic faith." [76] This last is an unusually modern statement of the case against propaganda in literature and it is rather a pity that Hazlitt did

mind, by submitting the shows of things to the desires of the mind; whereas reason doth buckle and bow the mind unto the nature of things."—Bk. II. iv. 2.

[75] "Pope, Lord Byron, and Mr. Bowles," *Works*, XI, 489 ff.

[76] "Charlemagne: ou l'Eglise Delivrée" (a review of Lucien Buonaparte's poem), *Works*, XI, 231.—This and occasional remarks of a similar nature show Hazlitt to have held a view which has attained great importance since his day in the development of the historico-social criticism of Taine and others. It is the idea that art develops out of the cultural environment even though it culminates in the work of individual genius. Hazlitt's account of Shakespeare's eminence as growing out from, though towering above, the high "table-land" of Elizabethan drama (*Works*, V, 180 ff.): his discussion, largely from Schlegel, of social and religious differences as contributing to classic and romantic art (*Works*, X, 78 ff.): his belief that Raphael and Michelangelo would not have painted the great pictures they did had they lived three hundred years later (*Works*, VI, 413–414): these are typical illustrations of the point.—A further account of this is given, p. 152 ff., below.

not develop the idea more fully. But another aspect of the
problem he does develop. He holds that the very disinterestedness of the true poet makes him the greatest of
moralists; his lack of an interested motive, that is, permits
him to exhibit truths undistorted, while religious bigots
and all those who wish to inculcate dogmas have in every
age "darkened knowledge." Poetry is nature moralizing
and idealizing for us, since by showing us things as they
are it teaches us, through sympathy, what they ought to
be. In this Shakespeare is contrasted with Shelley. The
former gives us nature and is the great moralist as well;
the latter starts out with doubtful speculative theories
(*Prometheus Unbound* is referred to) and proceeds to
"prove their truth by describing them in detail as matters
of fact." [77] But the poet's lesson should be inferential, derived from undoubted (vividly realized) facts, for the reason or understanding has given us many false beliefs in
the past, and cannot therefore set up to dictate to us with
the same authority as can human experience. "To embody an abstract theory, as if it were a given part of actual
nature, is an impertinence and indecorum." [78] Poetry,
though it may make us wiser and better men, has for its
aim not this but simply the giving of pleasure or "delight." [79]

It may be noted that whenever Hazlitt thinks of great
poetry, or of poetic genius, he then considers poetry in its
aspect of *truth* and not *escape*, for always with him genius
implies the power of seeing farther into the truth than

[77] Cf. his statement that "Shelley mistook the nature of the poet's calling,
which should be guided by involuntary, not by voluntary impulses."—
"Shelley's Posthumous Poems," *Works*, X, 256.

[78] "On People of Sense," *Plain Speaker, Works*, VII, 245–246.

[79] The subject of didactic literature is more fully discussed in connection
with the morality of the drama.—See p. 150 ff. below.

the common man can see. The degree to which Hazlitt's notion of genius agrees with that of Wordsworth has already been noticed. Coleridge had, indeed, some justification (from his philosophic standpoint) for the indignation expressed in a passage directed at the "pantheism" of Wordsworth and Hazlitt: [80] "But, surely, always to look at the superficies of objects for the purpose of taking delight in their beauty, and sympathy with their real or imagined life, is as deleterious to the health and manhood of intellect as always to be peering and unravelling contrivance may be to the simplicity of the affection and the grandeur and unity of the imagination." [81] Hazlitt in all his reflections on poetry and nature (except in his discussion of metre and poetic diction, which will be considered hereafter) is closer to Wordsworth than to Coleridge. Wordsworth in religion was no pantheist; but in his feeling as a poet there was, to Coleridge's infinite distress,[82] more than a suspicion of pantheism, and on this ground Hazlitt, though himself no professed pantheist, met him.

But on the subject of metre and poetic diction, notably the weakest, or at any rate the least adequately expressed, points in Wordsworth's theory of poetry, Hazlitt parts with him. Wordsworth's theory, Hazlitt recognizes, arose from "horror or contempt" of the abuses of what was known as poetic diction. But Hazlitt believes that there is actually no proper ground for controversy on this question, that the truth and common sense of the matter are so obvious as to preclude any reasonable argument.[83] There

[80] For Hazlitt's "pantheism" see the passage from "The Indian Jugglers," quoted on pp. 48–49, above.

[81] *Anima Poetae*. ed. E. H. Coleridge, New York, 1895. Entry under date of October 26, 1803, p. 29.

[82] Except perhaps in the earliest years of their friendship.

[83] I find that Mr. Howe in the notes to his new edition of Hazlitt considers that in this passage relating to common sense—but only up to this

is undoubtedly, he thinks, a simple and familiar language, common to almost all ranks of society through many ages, which is best adapted to the "direct expression of strong sense and deep passion, and which, consequently, is the language of the best poetry as well as of the best prose." There is also another language peculiar to poetry, "those flowers of speech," a glittering tissue "crusting over the rough stalk of homely thoughts," which has been the idiom of modern poetry. But it was also often the language of the greatest poets. It has a certain beauty and is not to be condemned in its place; but it is most proper to "descriptive or fanciful," that is, to the less intense kinds of poetry. Like classical diction, it is full of associations, not homely ones but distant, "sky-tinctured" ones, "dipped in 'the dew of Castalie.' " The literary associations of poetic diction, he thinks, are not to be scorned merely because they are literary, but only if they become a substitute for feeling instead of an expression of it as they have actually become in much of the fashionable poetry of the time.[84] It is on a similar basis that in a later lecture [85] Hazlitt justifies the weight of learning and the allusiveness of Milton's style: for all his borrowing, "the fervour of his imagination melts down and renders malleable" the great mass of material so that with him "learning has the effect of intuition."

Hazlitt's theory of metre marks a distinct advance over both Wordsworth's and Coleridge's. Recognition of the

point—"the pen is plainly held by Jeffrey." Neither the thought nor the style seems to me out of keeping with the rest of Hazlitt's writing. But the point is immaterial, since about the remainder of the article, which alone contains what is significant in the discussion, there is no question of Jeffrey's authorship (see Howe's edition, XVI, 134–135 and 426–427).

[84] "Coleridge's Literary Life." *Works*, X, 155–156.

[85] "On Shakespeare and Milton." *Lectures on the English Poets. Works*, V, 58–59.

subtle significance of the musical elements in poetry comes
as rather a surprise, indeed, from Hazlitt, for he seems to
have known and thought little about music as a separate
art. Wordsworth, it will be recalled, conceived that any
one possessing the other requisites of a poet, the powers,
that is, of "observation and description," of sensibility, reflection, imagination and fancy, invention, and judgement,
will "invariably" possess a "sensibility to harmony of
numbers, and the power of producing it." [86] This would
appear to most people something of a *non sequitur*. But indeed Wordsworth was hard pressed, as Coleridge pointed
out,[87] to find any place at all for metre in his theory of
poetry. The arguments by which he maintained that the
language of poetry should be a selection from the simple
language of simple people forced him to show cause why
the poet should not write prose instead, since metre at
once sets off poetry from common speech. His explanation
is that the pleasure we habitually associate with metre
serves, if the subject of the poem is painful or intense, to
calm the feelings so that an "overbalance" of pleasure will
be produced by the whole, and if the subject or the power
of expression in the poet is not so great, the presence of
metre will add to the general pleasure and raise it to a
higher pitch.[88] Wordsworth wrote more upon this subject,
and in later editions of the Preface he altered without improving the grounds of his defense of metre. A detailed
analysis of all his pronouncements on the subject cannot be
given here. The conclusion is inescapable, however, that
in theory at least, he did not get beyond the conception of
metre as something "superadded" to poetry, not an or-

[86] Preface to the 1815 edition of his *Poems*.
[87] *Biographia Literaria*, Chapter XVIII.
[88] Preface to the second edition of the *Lyrical Ballads*.

ganic part of it. Indeed, in the edition of 1832 he adds to the discussion in the Appendix the statement that "metre is but adventitious to composition."

Coleridge, in criticizing Wordsworth's theory of poetic diction (which is his real object of attack, and not Wordsworth's defense of metre) in the eighteenth chapter of the *Biographia Literaria* traces the origin of metre to "the balance in the mind effected by that spontaneous effort which strives to hold in check the workings of passion." [89] The impulse toward restraint, that which is artificial or voluntary, which creates the metre, is thus united as *will*, with passion, its opposite. This statement of Coleridge is beyond question an accurate expression of one part of the general function of form in art. But it is not, as he appears to assume, an account of the metrical as distinct from any other element of form. From this he proceeds to an account of the *effect* of metre, which is, he says, to "increase the vivacity and susceptibility both of the general feelings and of the attention," an effect which it produces by the quick though almost imperceptible alternations of curiosity gratified and re-excited. Metre, in fact, "in itself is simply a stimulant of the attention." The only answer he will give to the question why one should write sometimes in prose and sometimes in verse (that is, metrically) is this: "I write in metre, because I am about to use a language different from that of prose." [90] This and the customary associations which we have with metrical composition are its justifications.

Coleridge's account of metre is clearly an advance over Wordsworth's in that it recognizes metre as an element in form, and thus gives it a more organic relation to poetry

[89] Ed. Shawcross, II, 49.
[90] *Ibid.*, p. 53.

(form was always *organic* with Coleridge). But to a considerable degree metre is still, with him, something added from without, for the purpose of increasing the pleasure we take in beholding unity in diversity.

To Hazlitt the justification of metre is in its *expressiveness*. He saw that metre, or the music of verse, is not a mere external addition to a poem, but that form and substance are essentially one, or that they are as cause and effect to each other: "poetry is the music of language, expressing the music of the mind." He notes with approval an observation he has heard that "every one who declaims warmly or grows intent upon a subject, rises into a sort of blank verse or measured prose." It is worth noting, however, that for all his stress upon fidelity to nature Hazlitt does not fall into the error of resting the theory of metre upon this statement. According to his view, metre may be said to "imitate" or represent the real feeling, but not the real expression, of a person in a state of emotion. In the same way he escapes an almost identical error into which Schlegel falls (in a passage from the *Lectures on Dramatic Art and Literature* which Hazlitt quotes elsewhere, but without adopting all the ideas involved) on the subject of poetic diction. Schlegel has questioned Dr. Johnson's assertion that in Shakespeare the expression of pathos was not always natural and unaffected. Schlegel concedes a few passages in which "a too soaring imagination, a too luxuriant wit" remove the dialogue somewhat from complete verisimilitude. But in general he thinks the speech quite natural: for "energetical passions electrify the whole of the mental powers, and will, consequently, in highly favored natures, express themselves in an ingenious and figurative manner." [91] This is a half truth which becomes an error

[91] Quoted from Hazlitt's "Schlegel on the Drama," *Works*, X, 114.

when erected into a theory either in respect to poetic diction or in respect to metre. It is one which Hazlitt, with his inclination to think that the Elgin Marbles were casts from nature, might well have been expected to adopt, but did not. His theory is best expressed in his own words:

Whenever any object takes such a hold on the mind as to make us dwell upon it, and brood over it, melting the heart in love, or kindling it to a sentiment of admiration;—whenever a movement of imagination or passion is impressed on the mind, *by which it seeks to prolong and repeat the emotion, to bring all other objects into accord with it, and to give the same movement of harmony, sustained and continuous, to the sounds that express it* [italics mine],—this is poetry. The musical in sound is the sustained and continuous; the musical in thought and feeling is the sustained and continuous also. Whenever articulation passes naturally into intonation, this is the beginning of poetry. There is no natural harmony in the ordinary combinations of significant sounds: the language of prose is not the language of music, or of *passion:* and it is *to supply this inherent defect in the mechanism of language— to make the sound an echo to the sense, when the sense becomes a sort of echo to itself* [italics mine] . . . that poetry was invented.[92]

In this passage two ideas are strikingly combined. One is the recognition, related to Wordsworth's notion of poetry as springing from emotion recollected in tranquillity, of a distinction between the primary personal emotion and the same feeling when it has become the æsthetic one, when we seek *to prolong and repeat the emotion, to bring all other objects into accord with it.* It is this state of feel-

---

[92] "Coleridge's Literary Life," *Works*, X, 156–157.—The present discussion of Hazlitt's views on metre is based upon this article and the first of the *Lectures on the English Poets (Works*, V, 12 ff.) in which the same passage occurs with some alterations and additions. Once more it is notable what Hazlitt does in transforming the old formulas. "To make the sound an echo to the sense" is, of course, Pope's line, "The sound must seem an echo to the sense" (*Essay on Criticism*, line 365). But the meaning is different.

ing—*when the sense becomes a sort of echo to itself;* that is, when the emotion has become detached from the welter of personal feelings, has taken shape as the poet's vision— that the poet wishes to express by sounds which echo its rhythmical character.

Hazlitt thus sees not only what poetry gains by the use of rhythm, which might be an inorganic view of its function, but how prose actually hinders complete expression by fretting and diverting the mind with its stops and abruptnesses, and its "petty obstacles." Metre, then, is the truly *expressive* medium for poetic feeling.

An understanding of this passage is necessary as a supplement to Hazlitt's original definition of poetry as the impression of an object or event, exciting a movement of "imagination and passion, and producing, by sympathy, a certain modulation of the voice, or sounds, expressing it." By this definition feeling and form are already united, but the statement appears without a clear conception of the two kinds of emotion involved.

Hazlitt's account of the function of metre, though fundamentally sound, would have been strengthened (as would Wordsworth's and Coleridge's also) by a greater theoretical acquaintance with music. His statement that the musical in sound is "the sustained and continuous" appears to neglect the fact that it requires two alternating elements to produce rhythm; though it is still true that, as compared with prose, the *regularity* of those alternations produces an effect of sustained and continuous movement. Hazlitt's deficiency on this point, however, is rather one of terms than of ideas.

Upon one other controversy of the day—a less fruitful one, however—Hazlitt put in his word. The occasion was the publication of the first of Byron's letters to Murray

"On the Reverend William L. Bowles's Strictures on the Life and Writings of Pope." The discussion centers upon the question whether Pope was a poet and, further, whether *nature* or *art* is the more poetical or the better suited to be subject matter of poetry, Bowles upholding *nature,* and Byron *art* and Pope. There was some confusion over the meaning of *nature* and *art.* Bowles meant by *nature* both external nature and the passions of man, and contended that things of *art,* that is, objects made artificially by man for his own use, are poetical only insofar as *nature* has been joined to them by association. Byron, on the contrary, argues that objects in nature have no beauty or poetry in themselves but only as they are associated with the work of man—that a landscape painting of a natural scene must have its ruin to mark the hand of man.[93] Neither writer, however, is consistent in the meaning he attaches to the terms employed.

Hazlitt agreed essentially with Bowles in contending that the sun "is poetical *per se,*" no matter what it shines on; but he goes further in attempting to make clear the distinction between the terms *nature* and *art.* "By *art* and *artificial,* as these terms are applied to poetry or human life," he says, "we mean those objects and feelings which depend for their subsistence and perfection on the will and arbitrary conventions of man and society; and by nature, and natural subjects, we mean those objects which exist in the universe at large, without, or in spite of, the interference of human power and contrivance, and those interests and affections which are not amenable to the human will. . . . We are masters of Art, Nature is our master; and it is

[93] Byron, *Letters and Journals,* ed. Prothero, Vol. V. Appendix III. I am partially indebted in the discussion of this controversy to Powell, *op. cit.,* p. 44 ff.

to this greater power that we find working above, about, and within us, that the genius of poetry bows and offers up its highest homage." [94] *Art* is however not altogether excluded by Hazlitt as subject matter for poetry, any more than Pope, whose matter was always *art,* not *nature,* was excluded from the ranks of poets. As for Byron's ruin in a landscape, it is poetical, Hazlitt says, not because it is a work of art, "but because it is a work of art o'erthrown"; it calls to mind not what man's will has accomplished, but what greater forces have done in despite of man's will. Where the *artificial* flourishes and attains its object, imagination droops; for where all the wants and wishes are supplied by contrivance, "there can be no strong cravings after ideal good, nor dread of unimaginable evils; the sources of terror and pity must be dried up." [95] Real poetry, or poetry of the highest order, can be produced only by "unravelling the real web of associations, which have been wound round any subject by nature, and the unavoidable conditions of humanity." [96] Hence a candle (" 'How far that little candle throws its beams!' " Hazlitt quotes) though an object of *art,* is poetical when the thought of it is connected with darkness, silence, distance, or with privation or uncertain danger.

Yet there is, in Hazlitt's opinion, such a thing as a poet of *art* as well as of *nature;* or, if the name poet must be reserved for those of the highest order, at least there is no need to deny great merit to writers of another class. The poet of nature is one who, "from the elements of beauty, of power, and of passion in his own breast, sympathizes with whatever is beautiful, and grand, and impassioned in

---

[94] "Pope, Lord Byron, and Mr. Bowles," *Works,* XI, 498.
[95] *Ibid.,* pp. 496–497.
[96] *Ibid.,* p. 499.

nature," so that by the truth and depth and harmony of his mind he may be said to "hold communion with the very soul of nature, to be identified with, and to foreknow" the feelings of all men. "He sees things in their eternal beauty, for he sees them as they are; [97] he feels them in their universal interest; for he feels them as they affect the first principles of his and our common nature." [98] But because Pope was not in this sense a poet, we are not to think him nothing. He was the poet of *art,* with wit, sense, observation, "a quick *tact* for propriety of thought and manners" as established by society. So on this aspect of the controversy Hazlitt agrees with Byron, though for reasons somewhat different from Byron's, against Bowles.

Hazlitt's position in this discussion is another illustration of his abiding conviction that *excellence,* as well as truth, "is not one but many." Most great critics have maintained that a work must be judged according to its own laws and its own class—according, that is, to its own purpose. But few critics have been pluralistic in their philosophy (or in their psychology, as one sometimes feels that it should be called). Few have therefore maintained this critical principle in its application as consistently as did Hazlitt.

Drama

One of Hazlitt's greatest contributions to criticism has generally been reckoned his service in helping to establish the preëminence in our literature of Shakespeare and his contemporaries. In this he stands with Coleridge, Lamb,

[97] Here Hazlitt appears to be saying with Reynolds that *beauty* and *nature* are the same thing. The point, of course, is that always with Hazlitt the object is beautiful at least partly *because* it is *nature,* while with Reynolds it is beautiful because we have corrected it out of *nature.*

[98] "On the Question Whether Pope Was a Poet," *Works,* XI, 430–431.

and Schlegel. But Hazlitt did not appear to consider himself in the least a revolutionary in this work. The preface to *The Character of Shakespeare's Plays* opens with a quotation from Pope in praise of the verisimilitude of Shakespeare's characters. Shakespeare, Pope thinks, is "not so much an imitator, as an instrument of nature" which "speaks through him"; his characters are admirable for their life and variety, and for the consistency and individuality shown in the drawing of them. Hazlitt's expressed purpose in his book is "to illustrate these remarks in a more particular manner by a reference to each play." [99] This is but one more instance of what I have referred to as Hazlitt's tendency to pour new wine into the old bottles, to give a different significance to the "imitation of nature" without quarrelling with the formula itself. Even before he has got through the preface of his book, he expresses, without marking it, his real disagreement with Pope, for he says, in reference to the epithet "violets dim" from a favorite passage in the *Winter's Tale,* that Shakespeare's descriptions are "identical with the things themselves, seen through the fine medium of passion." But if he began with Pope on Shakespeare, he continued with Schlegel.

Although Hazlitt's treatment of individual authors as such—even of Shakespeare—does not form a part of our subject, there are some ideas contained in this first critical volume which are illustrative of his general views and should therefore be noticed. The first is the ground of his main disagreement with Schlegel.[100] The only ways in which he thought he might be able to improve upon the

[99] *Works,* I, 171.

[100] The general question of Hazlitt's relation to Schlegel and Coleridge in his Shakespearean criticism has already been discussed, p. 89 ff., above.

work of the German critic were "in avoiding an appearance of mysticism in his style" and in offering illustrations
of Shakespeare's greatness from particular passages in the
various plays, which the greater scope of Schlegel's lectures
precluded.[101] In this connection we must consider Hazlitt's review of Schlegel's work, already referred to, in
which he discusses at some length those points in which
he does or does not accede to the latter's views. But he
ranges here beyond the field of drama, and it will be necessary to follow him. After quoting a long introductory passage from the lectures containing, among other things,
Schlegel's definition of poetry (which is not Hazlitt's), Hazlitt proceeds to what he calls the "nucleus of the prevailing
system of German criticism, . . . namely, the essential
distinction between the peculiar spirit of the modern or
romantic style of art, and the antique or *classical*." [102] In
the lectures of Schlegel themselves this difference is
traced almost exclusively to the difference in religion.[103]
The religion of Greece was said to be a refined sensualism.
From a combination of fortunate circumstances in race
and situation the Greeks were possessed of a remarkable
harmony of all their faculties, and their poetry and art
were therefore expressions of joy in life. But the Christian
religion taught the antagonism between sense and spirit:
all was not harmony in this world. And therefore romantic
poetry was an expression of longing for past or future happiness, of attempted reconcilation of opposites.

In his survey of this portion of the work Hazlitt's departure from Schlegel is very marked. The clearest distinction
between the classic and romantic styles, he believes, lies

101 *Works*, I, 171–172.
102 "Schlegel on the Drama," *Works*, X, 81.
103 Schlegel's Lectures, I and XXII.

in the fact that the one is "conversant with objects that are grand or beautiful in themselves, or in consequence of obvious and universal associations; the other, with those that are interesting only by the force of circumstances and imagination." [104] He draws the contrast far less at the expense of the ancients than does Schlegel, who dwells at some length on the superiority of Christianity; and he avoids altogether what he calls Schlegel's "mysticism," the fervently religious tone of his championship of Christian-inspired art.[105] Hazlitt continues the contrast between the classic and the romantic as the poetry of "form" and the poetry of "effect," the poetry which gives only what is necessarily implied in a subject, and that which gives all that can possibly arise from it. He traces the difference not to religion alone but "perhaps" to "physical organization, situation, religion and manners." It is consistent with Hazlitt's usual avoidance of the subject of religion in his own works that he here minimizes as far as possible Schlegel's emphasis upon it.

As to his own taste in the drama, Hazlitt of course was almost purely a romantic. Though he was unwilling to assert, as Schlegel did in his first lecture, the great theoretical superiority of romantic art derived from a superior religion, yet when he came to treat the Greek drama specifically Hazlitt found Schlegel too much in awe of the classics, too much given to slavish admiration of them.[106] The true ground of Hazlitt's preference for the moderns is expressed in his comment on Sophocles in a passage

[104] *Op. cit.,* p. 81.
[105] Hazlitt's characteristic dislike of all that smacks of the mystic is almost too well shown by an odd juxtaposition of epithets, when he says that there is a great deal of "affectation and mysticism" in what the author says of Euripides.—*Ibid.,* p. 97.
[106] *Ibid.,* p. 88 ff.

which shows, incidentally, how far the theory of tragedy had travelled from neo-classic days. The plays of Sophocles, he says, "are hardly tragedies in our sense of the word," for they do not represent the extremes of passion and suffering. In modern tragedy the object is to represent the soul "utterly subdued as it were, or at least convulsed and overthrown" by misfortune or passion.[107] But in the classic drama of Sophocles firmness of purpose, calmness of sentiment are the chief qualities. "The mind is not shaken to its centre; the whole being is not crushed or broken down." The protagonist acts and suffers as if always in the presence of a higher power, "or as if human life itself were a religious ceremony." All is conducted with a fatal composure, all is prepared and submitted to with inflexible constancy.[108] As compared with Shakespeare the Greek dramatists, Hazlitt thinks, with all their genius, are both less individual and less universal in their portrayal of human beings: they seem to have given "only Greek manners and sentiments," whereas Shakespeare "described all the people that ever lived" with infinite variety and "perfect individuality." [109] Here Hazlitt shares the common romantic blindness to classic beauty. But this is possibly his most unfortunate expression of it; in other passages he shows a more just view of classic art, though always with a preference for the characteristic and the extreme over the abstractly beautiful and reposeful. The Elgin Marbles are the only productions of antiquity which roused him to a

[107] This statement needs to be qualified, however, by a truth which Hazlitt recognized in a later essay, that great tragedy always is to a certain degree "ideal," since it is "the superiority of character to fortune and circumstance, or the larger scope of thought and feeling thrown into it, that redeems it from the charge of vulgar grossness or physical horrors."—"The Ideal," *Works*, IX, 432.

[108] *Op. cit.*, p. 96.

[109] *Ibid.*, p. 112.

pitch of enthusiasm equal to that which he felt for Raphael or Shakespeare.

But it was not only in the classical or the French and English neo-classical drama that Hazlitt felt a lack of that truth which is to be found in the characteristic. Modern poets too, notably Byron in his drama, had got into the way of "scouting individuality as beneath the sublimity of their pretensions, and the universality of their genius." The persons in Byron's drama are no longer affected by particular incidents and feelings, but each declaims opinions on "fate, fortune, and the entire consummation of all things." The individual is not important enough either to himself or to the author. This, Hazlitt thinks, proceeds from a false estimate of individual nature and the value of human life: "we have been so used to count by millions of late, that we think the units that compose them nothing." He goes on, citing a passage from *The Duchess of Malfi* to show the value of the insight we gain into universal nature through this finely realized individual case. For in this respect "each man is a microcosm. What he is, the rest are." He is "an endless and infinitely varied repetition: and if we know what one man feels, we so far know what a thousand feel." Moral and poetical truth, therefore, are like expression in a painting—"the one is not to be attained by smearing over a large canvas, nor the other by bestriding a vague topic." [110] Hazlitt's recognition here of the principle of "unity in variety" is interesting for its relation to his philosophy. In general his emphasis was upon variety as Coleridge's was upon unity. Yet both recognized the other end of the antithesis, Hazlitt only rarely, Coleridge in the enunciation of his "principle of individuation," and in his frequent reiteration of the "principle of the reconciliation

[110] "On Reason and Imagination," *Plain Speaker, Works,* VII, 53–55.

of opposites." The two points of view unite in their ultimate application and in theory, but in *method* they remain
contrasted: hence Hazlitt's idea is that we learn by seeking
differences, by distinguishing; Coleridge's that we must
seek likenesses, must compare. This contrast, however,
should not be carried too far: if it were a perfect tempera-
mental antithesis, Coleridge must have preferred Greek
drama to Shakespeare, which he did not.

For a more general definition of what drama should be,
one may turn to a brief passage in *The Lectures on the
English Poets* in which Hazlitt marks the distinction between epic and drama. The former, he says, affects us
through the medium of imagination, by magnitude and
distance, by permanence and universality; it fills us with
admiration and delight: the latter affects us by sympathy
and nearness to us, fills us with terror and pity.[111] Or the
difference is this: that in the epic the imagination produces
the passion, while in the drama the passion produces the
imagination; the interest of the former arises from contemplation of objects in themselves grand and beautiful,
that of the latter from sympathy with the passions and
struggles of others.[112] The distinction as Hazlitt sees it
thus would seem to be, in terms of his comments on
Schlegel and romanticism, that the quality of epic poetry
is essentially classic, that of dramatic as a whole essentially
romantic. But again the antithesis is not complete, for he
goes on in the first passage to assert that dramatic and epic
poetry in their perfection "approximate to and strengthen
one another."

It is a pity that Hazlitt did not give a series of lectures
on the tragic writers, as he did on the comic writers and

---

[111] "On Shakespeare and Milton," *Works,* V, 52.
[112] "On the Character of Milton's Eve," *Works,* I, 110.

the poets. For in each of these series he set himself to the task of thinking out and stating in an introductory lecture which is invaluable for our purpose something of his theory of comedy and of poetry. He never did this for tragedy; yet if his natural sympathies and habitual interest favored any one form more than another it was this. It is possible, however, to arrive at some conclusions on this subject from his scattered criticism of poetry and drama.

In speaking of tragedy Hazlitt repeatedly quotes the Aristotelian maxim that it "purifies the affections by terror and pity," or, as he re-phrases it according to his own notions, "substitutes imaginary sympathy for mere selfishness." [113] But he goes further than this in later accounts (and in one earlier). His explanation of the pleasure afforded by tragedy, his answer to the question why we enjoy the sight or the vicarious experience of suffering on the stage as we do not in real life, is twofold. In the first place, he believes our pleasure has its root in "the common love of strong excitement." There is a natural inclination in the mind, a "desire to have its faculties roused and stimulated to the utmost." [114] He cites the observation made in Burke's essay *On the Sublime and Beautiful* [115] that, though people flock to see a fine tragedy, if word were brought of an execution going forth in the next street, the

[113] "Othello," *Characters of Shakespeare's Plays, Works,* I, 200.—In an article written about two years earlier, "On Modern Comedy" (*Round Table, Works,* I, 13) he gives a perhaps more superficial explanation of Aristotle's dictum—though the one above is perhaps not notable for depth—interpreting it to mean that tragedy "substitutes an artificial and intellectual interest for real passion." Hazlitt's casual explanation of Aristotle's "pity and terror" bears a close resemblance to that of Lessing. (Cf. Bosanquet's *History of Aesthetic,* p. 230 ff.) but probably was not derived, at least directly, from him.

[114] *Lectures on the English Poets,* I, *Works,* V, 7; and "On Mr. Kean's Iago," *Round Table, Works,* I, 15–16.

[115] Part I, section 15.

theatre would soon be empty. And he further notes that
hawkers of "full, true, and particular accounts of murders
and executions" do not need to have their news turned
into penny ballads to sell them. This feeling is generally
restrained and complicated in real life by a feeling of humanity and a sense of moral obligation, but it is none the
less present in us all. The desire to have our faculties
"stretched to the utmost" is either caused by or is identified
with the sense of power, which, as we have seen, Hazlitt
considered fundamental to the human constitution, and
which he regarded as power residing either in the self or
in the sense of the magnitude of another force outside the
self, or in both combined. Grandeur and sublimity result
from the contemplation of vast power outside the self; the
love of power in the self, "which is another name for
the love of mischief," [116] is seen at its height in such a character as that of Iago, in whom neither the principle of self-
interest nor that of self-preservation has much force, but
whose dominating motive is an almost æsthetic one, the
creation of evil, to satisfy the sense of power and the desire
for intensity of experience.

This is the first aspect of the problem of tragedy. The
aim of all high tragedy, Hazlitt says, is "to resolve the sense
of pain or suffering into the sense of *power* by the aid of
imagination, and by grandeur of conception and character." [117] The part played by imagination furnishes the
other element of tragedy, and this element is essentially, if
indirectly, a moral one. In proportion to the greatness of
the evil represented in tragedy is our sense and desire of
the opposite good aroused. The sufferings of the protagonist, by the force of contrast and through sympathy, arouse

[116] "On Mr. Kean's Iago," *Round Table, Works,* I, 15.
[117] "Conversations as Good as Real," *Works,* XII, 365.

in us a more than ordinarily intense vision of the good. That is, they enhance our "consciousness of the blessing, by making us sensible of the magnitude of the loss"; the storm of passion shows us the "rich depths of the human soul: the whole of our existence, the sum total of our passions and pursuits, of that which we desire and that which we dread, is brought before us by contrast; the action and re-action are equal; the keenness of immediate suffering only gives us a more intense aspiration after, and a more intimate participation with the antagonist world of good." [118] It endows us with a high and permanent interest beyond ourselves, for it "raises the great, the remote, and the possible to an equality with the real, the little and the near." [119]

This is the sum of what Hazlitt had to say on the subject of tragedy in general. One aspect of his theory, his idea that our sympathy with the protagonist is an identification with moral good, has perhaps not the psychological truth that he often displays. The incompleteness of his theory as a whole lies in the fact that, while recognizing the natural human desire to have our faculties stretched to the utmost, he failed to recognize the complementary truth, that this tension must after all be relieved, that the excitement requires for its completion repose. His theory and his personal taste are in this united (though whether one is cause of the other—and if so, *which*—it would be rash to say); for it is in the romantic drama that intensity predominates over repose, and in the classic—and this was the fault which Hazlitt, in different words, had to find with Sophocles—the repose is greater than the intensity. Yet Hazlitt

---

[118] "On Poetry in General," *Lectures on the English Poets. Works*, V, 6; and "Lear," *Characters of Shakespeare's Plays. Works*, I, 271–272.
[119] "Othello," *Ibid.*, p. 200.

was not utterly unmindful of this opposite principle of repose: it is implied in his statement that tragedy is always in some degree *ideal,* and in more concrete form it is implied in all Hazlitt's descriptions of Mrs. Siddons' acting of tragedy,[120] as well as in occasional comments on individual tragedies of Shakespeare.

For historical drama, which he considers rather as an adjunct to tragedy proper, Hazlitt confessed a distaste. In this he does not stand alone. Perhaps the most general and most valid ground for objection lies in the imperfections which adherence to fact necessarily entails from a purely formal standpoint. The plot, that is, can rarely be satisfactorily rounded out; and—a more subtle point, but one that is still a question of form if we are thinking in terms of organic form—the work cannot be sufficiently detached from all the extraneous associations which the historical material holds, to give the essential unity and disinterestedness to the whole. Hazlitt's objection to historical drama is not based upon this but upon an idea more characteristic of him and his interests. At the beginning of his account of *King John,* in *The Characters of Shakespeare's Plays*[121] he professes himself not sorry to have come to the end of the historical plays. He would rather indulge his imagination, he says, upon an imaginary theme; he would rather exercise his pity and terror upon fictitious danger and distress. "It gives a *soreness* to our feelings of indignation or sympathy, when we know that in tracing the progress of sufferings and crimes, we are treading upon real ground," that the end was a foregone conclusion, irrevocable, and placed beyond the reach of poetic justice.

---

[120] Especially in a paper published in the *Examiner* in 1828—"Mrs. Siddons." *Works,* XI, 381.

[121] *Works,* I, 306.—He says the same thing briefly elsewhere in regard to novels.—*Works,* I, 152; and III, 167.

The knowledge that the thing was really so, sharpens the pain and at the same time hangs a weight upon the imagination and is a drawback, therefore, on "the pleasure as well as the dignity of tragedy."

Though he considered tragedy a greater art than comedy, Hazlitt wrote much more about the latter from a theoretical standpoint than about the former. He has been said to be deficient in humor, and in certain points of view it is true of him. There is wit and often a brilliant, though scathing, irony in his own essays, but there is not much humor. Yet he was not devoid of it in the same sense that Milton and Wordsworth were, for the balance between the inner and the outer life were in him better—or at least more normally—maintained. And he was devoted to many of the greatest comic writers of the past, with perhaps a somewhat special sympathy for those of a satiric turn—to Rabelais, Cervantes, Swift, Sterne, and the Restoration dramatists.

The first of his *Lectures on the English Comic Writers,* "On Wit and Humour," is devoted wholly to an exposition of the problem of why we laugh and of what constitutes the different kinds and degrees of the laughable. The lecture is familiar to all readers of Hazlitt, yet no account of his æsthetic can pass over it too briefly.

The fashion for working out distinctions between such pairs of terms as *wit* and *humor,* or *fancy* and *imagination* goes back perhaps to Hobbes's neat definition of *judgement* as the power of distinguishing differences between similar things, and *fancy,* or *wit,* as the power of seeing similarities in dissimilar things.[122] This definition was taken up by Locke, and was passed on through Dryden and Addison. Almost an epidemic of such definitions followed. *Taste*

122 Bosker, *op. cit.,* p. 29.

was distinguished from *genius,* the *sublime* from the
beautiful, and so on. The original definition of Hobbes
was repeated along with these quite generally down to the
time of Coleridge, who in his lectures delivered in the
winter of 1818 rephrased it. It is from the intellectual
operation of detecting the identity in dissimilar things, he
says, that *wit* arises, and adds further that the identity may
be in thought, in words, or in images—in which last case
it is more often called fancy.[123] Hazlitt, as will appear, de-
parted from the current idea. His first undertaking in the
lecture "On Wit and Humour," however, was to explain
the psychological basis of laughter and to define the laughable. "Man is the only animal that laughs and weeps," he
says, "for he is the only animal that is struck with the difference between what things are, and what they ought to
be." Our tears are shed for what thwarts our desires in
"serious matters" (a somewhat question-begging expression perhaps); our laughter arises from that which sur-
prises or disappoints our expectation in trifles.[124] The
discontinuous in our sensations produces a corresponding
jar or convulsive movement of the body, which will be
laughter unless there is involved at the same time a threat
to our safety or interest or happiness. Our habitual frame
of mind is a serious one in which the mind lays emphasis
upon expectation of a given course of events. The ludicrous or comic arises when the stress or concentration of
this forward gaze of expectation is suddenly relaxed by a
break in the chain of events. The essence of the laughable
is, then, he believes, "the incongruous, the disconnecting
one idea from another, or the jostling of one feeling

[123] Coleridge, *Miscellanies, Æsthetic and Literary,* p. 121.
[124] *Lectures on the English Comic Writers. Works,* VIII, 5.

against another." [125] This accounts for all forms of humor, from the crudest to the most subtle, from the *ludicrous,* which is a contradiction between the object and our expectation, heightened by its being contrary to the customary or the desirable—from this to the *ridiculous,* which is the highest degree of the laughable because it is contrary not only to custom but to sense and reason as well. The ridiculous is properly the province of satire.[126]

From the standpoint of presentation in literature, *humor* is said to be description of the ludicrous "as it is in itself," whereas *wit* goes further and exposes its object by comparison or contrast with something else. The humor of literature is "an imitation of the natural or acquired absurdities of mankind, or of the ludicrous in accident, situation, and character"; but *wit* illustrates or heightens the effect of that absurdity by a sudden and unexpected likeness or opposition, "which sets off the quality we laugh at or despise in a still more contemptible or striking point of view." [127] Or, as he expresses the distinction in an account of Hudibras: [128] "Humour is the making others act or talk absurdly and unconsciously: wit is the pointing out and ridiculing that absurdity consciously, and with more or less ill-nature." *Wit* is thus *humor,* with the comment of the observing mind super-added.[129]

Hazlitt takes pains to point out his departure from the

[125] *Ibid.,* p. 7.
[126] *Ibid.,* p. 8.
[127] *Ibid.,* p. 15.
[128] *Lectures on the English Poets,* IV, *Works,* V, 83.
[129] In another detached essay ("Definition of Wit," *Works,* XII, 445 ff.) Hazlitt treats this topic in a somewhat more elaborate fashion, but with the same essential idea as that given here. The association of ill-nature with wit has its precedents. Professor Allardyce Nicoll (*The Theory of Drama,* p. 194 n.) traces the notion of the comic as fundamentally malicious through Hobbes, Molière, and Jonson back to Plato.

accepted definition of wit, the currency of which he attributes to Locke, quoting a passage from Locke's *Essay* and
another from Hobbes's *Leviathan*,[130] and then introducing instances of wit which does not arise from likeness, as
well as citing James Harris's opinion that the demonstration of the equality of the three angles of a right triangle
to two right angles would, upon the principle of Locke,
constitute wit. Hazlitt marks wit as distinct from poetry
by the fact that it comes from imagination "inverted" and
so applied as "to make the little look less, the mean more
light and worthless; or to divert our admiration or wean
our affections from that which is lofty and impressive, instead of producing a more intense admiration and exalted
passion, as poetry does." [131] There is a wit of words and
of things,[132] but it is not always easy to distinguish between the two; and there is also "a wit of sense and observation, which consists in the acute illustration of good
sense and practical wisdom, by means of some far-fetched
conceit or quaint imagery." [133] Finally, *irony*, is a species
of wit which owes its effect to the contrast between the
appearance and the reality.[134]

So much for definitions and distinctions. But there is
more to the interpretation of comic effect than this. There
is, for instance, the matter of *keeping* in character, which
is perhaps the highest development of the comic. It is
"consistency in absurdity" as we find it in *Don Quixote*,
for instance—a "determined and laudable attachment to

---

[130] *Lectures on the Comic Writers, Works*, VIII, 18 n.

[131] *Ibid.*, p. 15.

[132] *Ibid.*, p. 21. Cf. Coleridge's statement that the identity to which wit
calls attention may be identity in thought, in words, or in images.—Passage
cited on p. 142, above.

[133] *Ibid.*, p. 24.

[134] *Ibid.*, p. 10.

the incongruous and singular." This truth of absurdity to itself, while it heightens the comic effect, at the same time softens and harmonizes its excesses: "the ludicrous is here blended with a certain beauty and decorum, from this very truth of habit and sentiment, or from the principle of similitude in dissimilitude," [135] as Hazlitt expresses it in a somewhat Coleridgean phrase. It is therefore comedy most perfectly moulded into the form of art.

Upon the more specific matter of the comic drama Hazlitt had a good deal to say, and in particular he had a favorite theory to account for the decline of modern comedy. The theory was first developed at length in two letters contributed to the *Morning Chronicle* in 1813,[136] and it reappears in the eighth of the lectures. In the account of *Twelfth Night* in his *Characters of Shakespeare's Plays* Hazlitt had marked out three stages in the history of English comedy, stages which he evidently considered to be the normal ones in the development of comedy in any society.[137] The first is that in which the idiosyncrasies and follies of individuals are "of nature's planting," rather than the results of social environment. The individuals are unconscious of their deviation from what is usual, or if they are aware of it, they do not care so long as they

[135] *Ibid.*, p. 11.

[136] One of these is to be found in the Appendix to Volume VIII of Hazlitt's *Works;* the other Hazlitt himself inserted in the *Round Table* (*Works,* I, 10) as a paper "On Modern Comedy." Hazlitt's theory of the decline of comedy was one of the ideas which Coleridge claimed as his: he had a "distinct recollection of having conversed the greater part of it (that is, of the first of these letters) at Lamb's."—Coleridge's *Letters,* II, 615–616.— Like some other questions of priority and indebtedness which involve Coleridge, it must remain unsettled. The point is taken up by Howe (*Life,* 155 n.), who adds that he thinks it "conceivable that the reader may have grown somewhat tired of Coleridge's endeavours, having ruined his own career, to prevent Hazlitt from having one."

[137] *Works,* I, 313.

"can but have their whim out." Since they are not attempting to impose pretensions upon others, the spectator
receives pleasure from humoring them rather than from
exposing their absurdity. This Hazlitt calls "the comedy
of nature." It is the comedy most often to be found in
Shakespeare. The second stage is that best represented by
the Restoration dramatists, the comedy of manners. In the
society which this represents men become aware of their
peculiarities, affect to disguise their real selves, and set up
pretensions to what they are not. Comedy then has for its
object the removal of these disguises, the holding up of
vanity and the "preposterous assumptions" of self-love to
detection and ridicule. It is the comedy of artificial life, of
wit, and satire. But finally, with a more general diffusion
of knowledge of the world and of books, and as a result
too of seeing affectation so long exposed upon the stage,
there comes a period when the materials of comic character are neutralized and there is no comedy left—or only
the *sentimental,* which is as good as none.

It is clear from a number of passages in his work that,
though Hazlitt distinguishes three types of comic drama,
he considers, for some unfathomable reason, that the true
province of comedy lies in the second of these—he believes that comedy is essentially a matter of detection and
exposure, and that other types are mere variants, aber-
rations from the normal, however fine some of them may
be.[138] This attitude, though somewhat unaccountable,

---

[138] There is one passage, however, in which Hazlitt contradicts his own
more frequently expressed opinion on this point. In remarks prefaced to
Colman's *The Jealous Wife* in Oxberry's *New English Drama,* Vol. I (also
quoted in Hazlitt's *Works,* VIII, 505, note to page 163), written a short time
after the *Lectures on the English Comic Writers,* he says: "Congreve's
comedies for the most part are satires . . . The best and most genuine
kind of comedy, because the most dramatic, is that of character or humour,
in which the persons introduced upon the stage are left to betray their own

does itself account for what occasionally appears an under-valuation of Shakespeare's comedies in Hazlitt's writing. In the passage on *Twelfth Night* just cited he calls this play one of the most delightful of them, though "it is per-haps too good-natured for comedy." It has "little satire and no spleen": it "aims at the ludicrous rather than the ridiculous." It causes us to laugh at the follies of mankind but not to despise them. Indeed Shakespeare seems anxious to show his comic characters in the most favorable light rather than to render them contemptible.[139] Hazlitt always considered Shakespeare supreme in tragedy, but not in comedy.[140] In the second of the *Lectures on the Comic Writers* he expresses the opinion that in the realm of comedy Rabelais and Cervantes excelled Shakespeare, one in "the power of ludicrous description, the other in the invention and perfect keeping of comic character," and that Molière was at least as great as he. Over and over again, the very humanity of Shakespeare's genius and his poetic imagination Hazlitt sees as standing in the way of his comic sense. After quoting the dialogue between Shallow and Silence on "old Double's" death he remarks:

The reader laughs (as well he may) in reading the passage, but he lays down the book to think. The wit, however divert-ing, is social and humane. But this is not the distinguishing characteristic of wit, which is generally provoked by folly, and spreads its venom upon vice.

The fault, then, of Shakespeare's comic Muse is, in my opinion, that it is too good-natured and magnanimous. [141]

folly by their words and actions." Yet even here the purpose of comedy is still seen to be the *betraying* of folly.

[139] See also *Lectures on the English Comic Writers*, II. *Works*, VIII, 31–32.

[140] On one occasion, it is true, he remarks that Shakespeare "had an equal genius for comedy and tragedy: and his tragedies are better than his comedies, because tragedy is better than comedy."—*Lectures on the English Poets*, III. *Works*, V, 56.

[141] *Works*, VIII, 34–35.

Shakespeare's characters were for the most part "a kind of
grotesques, or solitary excrescences growing up out of
their native soil without affectation, and which he under-
took kindly to pamper for the public entertainment." [142]
His view of Shakespearean comedy as a whole is summed
up in another passage:

> I do not, in short, consider comedy as exactly an affair of
> the heart or the imagination; and it is for this reason only
> that I think Shakespeare's comedies deficient. I do not, how-
> ever, wish to give a preference of any comedies over his. . . .
> Finally, I will not say that he had not as great a natural genius
> for comedy as any one; but I may venture to say, that he
> had not the same artificial models and regulated mass of
> fashionable absurdity or elegance to work upon.[143]

Comedy, in its proper sense, according to Hazlitt, then,
is to be found in "the distinguishing peculiarities of men
and manners"; but the distinction can subsist, "so as to be
strong, pointed, and general," or at least its comic harvest
is richest, only at a moment in society after individual
infirmities have passed into general manners, but before
all distinctions are wiped out. The country squire must
still be a different species from the fine gentleman, the
citizen from the courtier. Everyone must have been aping
everyone else, but we must still be able clearly to perceive
which is ape and which genuine.[144]

In saying that we no longer have material in life for

---

[142] *Ibid.,* p. 36.

[143] *Ibid.,* p. 38.

[144] *Ibid.,* p. 36–37 and Lecture VIII, *ibid.,* p. 150.—It may be noted that
the reason which Hazlitt gives, here and in the following paragraph, for
the decline of comedy—the levelling of human differences, that is, by ex-
ternally applied uniformity—is precisely the same as the reason given by
Hugh Blair for the superiority of English over French comedy (in *Lectures
on Rhetoric and Belles Lettres,* Lecture 47). It is not certain whether
Hazlitt had read Blair or not.

comedy Hazlitt is not implying that the world is quite re-
formed, or even well on its way to a moral Utopia. The
amount of absurdity and prejudice and perversity in the
world has not been diminished; we are no doubt as foolish as ever and as egotistical. Only we keep our follies to
ourselves as far as we can: "we palliate, shuffle, and equivo-
cate with them; they sneak into bye-corners, and do not,
like *Chaucer's Canterbury Pilgrims,* march along the high
road, and form a procession; they do not entrench themselves strongly behind custom and precedent; they are not
embodied in professions and ranks in life; they are not
organized into a system." We are "no longer rigid in
absurdity, passionate in folly"; and, perhaps worst of all,
we anticipate ridicule by laughing (feebly, no doubt) at
our follies ourselves.[145] It is Hazlitt's belief, therefore, that
comedy inevitably wears itself out, "destroys the very food
on which it lives." Thus once again the theory that the
arts are not progressive is vindicated.[146]

The old canons of French classical drama, which had
dominated English critical thought in the eighteenth
century, had, by the time Hazlitt began to write dramatic
criticism, come to be largely disregarded by the dramatists,
though they still figured in critical controversy. Hazlitt
expends no great energy in quarrelling with them. He
refers to the unities now and then; he approves Schlegel's

[145] *Ibid.,* p. 151.
[146] *Ibid.,* p. 149.—He does not believe in the possibility of development
of a more subtle comedy dealing with finer, more minute distinctions, such
as has in fact been accomplished in fiction since Hazlitt's day by Meredith.
But throughout this discussion Hazlitt is clearly thinking of comedy only
as drama, even though elsewhere he uses the term in relation to fiction as
well. The material of comedy must be more or less plain, palpable, and
broad in outline, or it will not tell on the stage. Hazlitt sees therefore no
possibility of refining upon distinctions of character in comedy without
becoming trivial.—*Works,* VIII, 554-555 (Appendix I.)

insistence upon the necessity of judging each kind of drama according to its own nature instead of judging the romantic by the laws of classic drama; he justifies Shakespeare's indulgence of the nonsense of fools in serious plays as extreme relaxation from extreme tension.[147] But he does not enter the old dramatic controversy at full tilt. This was very likely because he was himself such an ardent playgoer. The modern plays that he saw at Covent Garden or Drury Lane were not as a rule bound to the unities, and the discussion over these laws may well have seemed to Hazlitt almost a dead issue.

The question of the use of drama for moral preachment is, however, perennial, and on this Hazlitt's opinion is interesting. It may be seen from what has already been said of his views on comedy that in this phase of drama a moral result, in some degree, if not a moral intention, is accepted. And on tragedy, too, his statement that our apprehension of the magnitude of the present evil excites in us a desire for and an admiration of the opposite good, attaches the drama to morality. He is none the less definitely opposed to anything which might be called moralistic drama, and he gives his reasons.

The moral comedies of Steele he condemns on the ground that they make both virtue and vice unreal. The comic writer should "open the volume of nature and the world for his living materials, and not take them out of his ethical common-place book." His most complete statement on this point is made in regard to prose fiction, but it applies equally to the drama and other forms of literature that may be drawn to didacticism. The most moral writers, he says, are those

147 "Merry England," *Works*, XII, 22.

who do not pretend to inculcate any moral: The professed
moralist almost unavoidably degenerates into the partisan of
a system; and the philosopher warps the evidence to his own
purpose. But the painter of manners gives the facts of human
nature, and leaves us to draw the inference: If we are not
able to do this, or do it ill, at least it is our fault.[148]

Hazlitt is "as little for introducing the tone of the pulpit or reading-desk on the stage, as for introducing plays
and interludes in church-time." [149] The stage indeed is the
best teacher of morals, but only because it is "the truest
and most intelligible picture of life." [150] His view of
morality in drama is thus identical with that indicated in
his criticism of Shelley's *Prometheus Unbound* as being
founded upon a philosophical theory instead of upon
"nature." [151]

On this question Hazlitt would seem to be of the same
opinion as Coleridge were it not that the difference of
emphasis between the two is almost great enough to
amount to a difference in theory. Coleridge's analysis in
the *Biographia Literaria* [152] of the immediate and the
ultimate aims of poetry as being, respectively, pleasure,
and moral or intellectual truth, is fairly parallel with
Hazlitt's idea that the imitation of nature, which gives us
æsthetic pleasure, is the proper province of poet and
dramatist, and that if he accomplishes this, one result beyond the pleasure will (or may) be an uplifting of our
moral sense. But the degree to which Coleridge ignored
his own theory is brought out in two letters to Sir Hum-

---

[148] "Standard Novels and Romances," *Works*, X, 27.
[149] *Lectures on the Comic Writers*, VIII, *Works*, VIII, 157.
[150] "On Actors and Acting," *Round Table, Works*, I, 153.
[151] P. 120, above.
[152] Chapter XIV.

phrey Davy, of October 9, 1800, and February 3, 1801, written, it will be observed, at a time when the philosopher and moralist in him had by no means yet eclipsed the poet. He speaks of his plan to write a life of Lessing and an essay on poetry. "The latter is still more at my heart than the former: its title would be an essay on the elements of poetry,—it would be in reality a disguised system of morals and politics." In the second letter it has become an essay " 'Concerning Poetry, and the nature of the Pleasures derived from it.' I have faith that I do understand the subject, and I am sure that if I write what I ought to do on it, the work would supersede all the books of metaphysics, and all the books of morals too." [153]

What interests Hazlitt is primarily the pleasure, and what interests Coleridge is preëminently the moral; and so their paths in criticism are quite divergent. For this reason, although moral benefit could hardly be expected to result from Restoration comedy,[154] yet Hazlitt considers this the great period of English comic writers, while Coleridge condemns it outright. Hazlitt thus approaches the drama frankly as an æsthetic experience altogether and in this he is more modern—despite the backward glances of our "new Humanists"—and more sound—despite the same professors—than any other important critic. He might, if he had wished, have justified his acceptance of the moral code upon which Restoration comedy rested, by his belief, quoted in these pages once before, that "whatever appeals to the imagination, ought to rest on undivided sentiment, on one undisputed tradi-

---

[153] *Letters,* I, 338 and 347.

[154] Yet Lamb says: "I feel the better always (and he is speaking of morals) for the perusal of one of Congreve's—nay, why should I not add even of Wycherley's comedies!" This is in his essay "On the Artificial Comedy of the Last Century."

tion, one catholic faith," [155] and that to produce great works of art the mind of the individual genius must "co-operate" with "the mind of the age or country." [156] Hazlitt himself would not—and did not—hold the same standards of morality as subsisted in the age of Charles II. But he knew that the literature of the time reflected that life, and he believed that great literature never does anything else.

This idea that great art can arise only out of a unified and homogeneous culture, and that genius can do its best work only when it is affirming and not denying its origin and environment, is an instance of a broader historical understanding than Hazlitt has been given credit for. It is an idea which Matthew Arnold took up in a somewhat different way in his criticism of Hazlitt's own contemporaries. In still more recent times, particularly in America with the expatriation of Henry James and of the many American writers after him, it has become a major question in our criticism. It has even furnished the basis for most of the contemporary development of what we are calling "sectionalism" in literature. And, as is well known, it has played an important part in the work of George Moore, Yeats, and others in the attempt to develop a richer and more vital art for modern times, especially for Ireland.[157] Hazlitt, and—so far as the writer is aware—no one else in his day, recognized the importance of this *rapport* between the artist and his environment. He had more to say on this point, the substance of which was that we must accept the present and do what we can in it. If there are no Shakespeares now, "there is a change

---

[155] "Charlemagne: ou l'Eglise Delivrée," *Works*, XI, 234.
[156] *Conversations of Northcote, Works*, VI, 413-414.
[157] See, for example, the chapter "Nationality in Art" in Moore's *Modern Painting*, and scattered passages in his *Hail and Farewell;* also, Yeats's "Ireland and the Arts" and "The Galway Plains" in his *Essays*.

in the world, and we must conform to it. Instead of striving to revive the spirit of Old English literature, which is impossible, unless we could restore the same state of things, and push the world back two centuries in its course, let us add the last polish and fine finish to the modern *Belles-Lettres.*" We still have more of the old books and old pictures than we shall ever be able to read as it is. We should continue to enjoy them without repining; but we should not attempt in our own work to imitate them, for between them and us lies a "gulph of ever-rolling years." We should follow our own line: if we are superficial, let us at least be brilliant in our superficiality. We must, whether we would or not, yield to the spirit of the age.[158] This is, incidentally, Hazlitt's best argument, though it is one he rarely directed in that way, against Sir Joshua Reynolds's excessive emphasis upon the desirability of imitating the work of the great masters in preference to imitating nature. And it justifies the practice of the Restoration dramatists as well. For there must be a correspondence in "manners, passions, religion," between a genius and his times. A single mind cannot move "in direct opposition to the vast machine of the world around it; . . . the poet can do no more than stamp the mind of his age upon his works." [159] Thus, though Hazlitt himself had not the scholarship necessary to pursue the historical method of criticism, he clearly saw that the productions of genius are not isolated phenomena but are in part the result of relationship and environment. This is a notable

---

[158] "The Periodical Press," *Works*, X, 202–209.

[159] "On Thomson and Cowper," *Lectures on the English Poets, Works,* V, 96. This last statement must, of course, be taken in the light of his conception of genius as the power of seeing farther into truth than others see, or as the power of discovering "new and valuable truth."

achievement in a so-called romantic critic who is expected
to stick to the creed of individualism for good or ill.[160]
   The history of theatrical, apart from dramatic, criticism
has yet to be written; but when it is, Hazlitt will be found
to have played an important part in it. From the standpoint of his æsthetic, the most important contribution of
this part of his writing lies in his recognition of the degree
to which the perfection of the art of acting passes beyond
mere "imitation of nature." Reading through the majority
of his passing reviews of the plays given night by night,
one finds most often reiterated expressions of the "perfect
truth and nature" in one actor's performance or of the
lack of it in another's. In these criticisms the theory of
acting assumed appears to have gone no further than that
of pure, literal *imitation,* though even here it is at least
always imitation by sympathy and feeling. But when he
wrote of Mrs. Siddons, or when upon occasion he under-
took to explain why Kean, though perhaps the greatest
actor then on the stage, was yet inferior to her, he recognized a different principle. Mrs. Siddons, he said, represented a character with perfect truth and sympathy; she
could touch all the chords of human passion, she possessed
the utmost force combined with the utmost variety of
expression; her transitions were rapid and extreme. Yet
these extremes of her acting were always "massed into
unity and breadth"; even as the passions thrilled through
her she yet preserved an elevation of thought and character above them. Whatever part she might be playing, she
"wore a crown" and "walked the earth in majesty and
pride." [161] Kean's acting was also very fine (Kean was in a

160 For this see also p. 119, above.
161 "Mrs. Siddons," *Works,* XI, 382–383.

sense Hazlitt's discovery, and the latter was never tired of praising him) but Hazlitt would have him go on to something still greater: there should be more "internal emotion" and a greater stateliness, a "measured march" added to "infinite force and truth, that he may be the greatest poet, as he unquestionably is the greatest prose-actor of the stage." It is a lack of this that keeps him inferior to Mrs. Siddons.[162]

Lamb is remembered as observer of the fact that the good comic actor does more than impersonate the fool whose part he plays, that by his manner he comments upon the character, that he takes the audience into the secret with him.[163] Hazlitt had earlier said something of nearly the same sort in regard to the part of Bob Acres in *The Rivals*. The character is in a sense not real but is prompted by Sheridan and tutored into absurdity. This the actor must realize and reproduce also: he must "humour the extravagance, and seem to take a real and cordial delight in caricaturing himself."[164]

From this it is clear that Hazlitt sees the art of acting as an art, like any other, in which the purpose is to represent "truth" and "nature," through the medium of the artist's imagination. It is no more than this that constitutes the principle of most modern "æsthetic" criticism of acting in such writers as Stark Young and others. To readers of this school Hazlitt's idea must seem a platitude; but we in general scarcely realize to what a degree even of late years the thoughtless theory of pure imitation has clung

---

[162] "Kean's Macbeth," *Works*, XI, 405.

[163] In the essay on "Stage Illusion," from the *Last Essays of Elia*. This essay was first published in 1825.

[164] From the prefaces to Oxberry's *New English Drama*, quoted in Hazlitt's *Works*, VIII, 508–509. This is from the first volume of Oxberry, which was published in 1818.

to the interpretive arts (those of acting and musical per-
forming) even though it is abandoned or re-defined in the
admittedly creative arts. In his theatrical criticism Hazlitt
will be found to be more aware of questions of form—of
wholeness and "keeping" throughout a part, of transitions
and unity of effect—than he is in most of his other
criticism.[165]

Style—Criticism

On the question of style, whether in literature or in the
representative arts, Hazlitt has a good deal to say in one
way and another, though most of it has little relation to
his general æsthetic views. "Style," he says, "properly
means the mode of representing nature; and this again
arises from the various character of men's minds, and the
infinite variety of views which may be taken of nature." [166]
More specifically in relation to literature he states that
style is "the adaptation of words to things." [167] This ranges
him clearly with Coleridge, Wordsworth, and De Quincey [168] (but more unequivocally than the last two) as opposed to the idea of style as an external adornment, or
something superadded, as Arnold later considered it to
be. He emphasizes more than does Coleridge the extent
to which the "variousness of men's minds" makes for
variousness of style, seeing as usual principles of diversity
while Coleridge seeks for unity.

Certain other of Hazlitt's opinions on style have exerted

[165] This is illustrated by such passages as that in which he describes
Charles Kemble's playing of Hamlet as done with too "determined in-
veteracy of purpose," and "in one undeviating straight line."—*Works*, XI,
207.
[166] "Flaxman's Lectures on Sculpture," *Works*, X, 344.
[167] *Works*, I, 421 (note to p. 42).
[168] Coleridge, *Miscellanies Æsthetic and Literary*, p. 182; and Powell,
op. cit., p. 173 ff.

their influence. The best known of these, his account of
"familiar style," contains the seed—almost, indeed, the full-
grown doctrine—of the best modern teachings about prose
style. And in the same essay Hazlitt anticipated the later
doctrine of *le mot juste,* though he failed to illustrate it
with cab-horses.[169] Familiar too is his difference of opinion
with Coleridge on the prose style of poets, the latter main-
taining that their sense of metre makes them good prose
writers,[170] Hazlitt that from the very freedom of the prose
medium they find themselves at a loss.[171] But all these
points belong to the study of Hazlitt's literary criticism
considered in itself rather than in its relation to his
æsthetic and philosophy.

Much has been written, since Matthew Arnold so greatly
increased our awareness of the problem, about the function of the critic and criticism in literature, and about
the proper basis for critical judgments. The division between intuitivists and dogmatists has become fairly
marked. In Hazlitt's time the assumptions of the older and
still dominant ´school of criticism, as represented in the
influential reviews and magazines, were still those of
Dr. Johnson's day: roughly speaking, the laws of composition in every species were considered to be already known,
and the function of the critic was therefore to measure all
new productions by these laws. Hazlitt, Lamb, Leigh
Hunt, and to some extent De Quincey, are thought of as
the chief exemplars in this age of the other, the intuitive

---

[169] "On Familiar Style," *Works,* VI, 242-48. For other remarks on prose
style, see XI, 195, 335; VII, 275; and numerous passages elsewhere.

[170] Lecture on Style, 1818. *Miscellanies Æsthetic and Literary,* p. 181.

[171] "On the Prose Style of Poets," *Plain Speaker, Works,* VII, 5 ff. Wordsworth's opinion is also recorded on this point. In a conversation that took
place in 1846 he "agreed to the saying that all great poets write good prose;
he said there was not one exception."—*Wordsworth's Literary Criticism*
(ed. N. C. Smith), p. 252.—The controversy appears to have had a fairly
long life—or perhaps Wordsworth a long memory for an injury.

or romantic criticism, with Coleridge standing somewhere
between, rejecting the old canons of criticism but believing in the establishment of new ones which are to be
created and exercised not by *reason* in the sense of
eighteenth-century rationalism, but by Reason in a (more
or less) Platonic sense, which combines in some measure
these other faculties but which is both more than and
different from either, in that it is also an independent
source of knowledge of Truth and the Absolute.[172]

Probably no critic can be wholly intuitive in his
method. But that Hazlitt was less unreservedly so than is
generally supposed, it has been one purpose of this study
to show. It remains to indicate briefly what Hazlitt himself thought of the function of criticism; and this, it may
be said, is one of the most impressionistic aspects of his
thought, largely because it leads back, of necessity, to his
indecision on the question of taste. It will be recalled that,
like most other writers, he found himself unable to hold
firmly either to the conviction that there is an absolute
standard of taste discoverable by the operation of judgement; or the contrary notion that taste is after all literally
taste, and that one man's preference is therefore as good
or as valid as another's. It is the dilemma of every critic
and every philosophy of art. Some critics, like Coleridge,
have tended to support the first alternative in theory, and
to apply the second in practice (this is true of Coleridge at
least when his individual criticisms are at their best).
Others have tried to hold largely to the first both in theory
and practice; and in general their specific criticisms have
suffered in consequence. This was the case with such
widely different writers as Johnson and Arnold. Hazlitt

---

[172] In his concrete criticism of specific works, of course, Coleridge is
ranged with the other romantic critics.

certainly fared no better than these. But the very leeway
which his pluralistic philosophy and æsthetic gave, he
turned to advantage in working back and forth from
theory to practice with less friction.

At the same time, Hazlitt had no very exalted opinion
of the race of critics in general. Even apart from his dia-
tribes against Gifford and others, "little men in high
places," he rarely considered the critic as much more than
a reviewer of books. In his essay "On Criticism" in the
volume of *Table-Talk* [173] he explains that the flood of
writing which issues from the modern press is too large to
cope with, and that we must therefore have *"tasters* for
the public, who must have a discretionary power vested
in them, for which it is difficult to make them properly
accountable." This point is followed up with a good deal
of spleen against the abuse of the reviewer's power, though
Hazlitt has no remedy to offer for the situation. He objects
to the petty "political" school of critics. He objects also
to the eighteenth-century English criticism which derived
its formulas from the French classicists. These, he says,
discuss nothing but "the superficial plan and elevation, as
if a poem were a piece of formal architecture": the plot,
the moral, the method are all, the genius nothing. What
has been called the school of Taste,[174] eighteenth-century
critics who were in one or two slight respects precursors of
romantic criticism, and a pale reflection of whose work
was to be found in such a publication as the *Monthly Review,* Hazlitt treats with a kindly tolerance of their amia-

---

[173] *Works*, VI, 214 ff.

[174] See, for example, Bosker, *op. cit.*, Chapter XIII. This refers to critics
who, like Goldsmith, Shenstone, and Blair, accepted for the most part the
canons of reason or common sense, but who were aware of the presence in
art of an appeal to something else than this, which they rather loosely referred to as *taste.*

ble inanities upon "an agreeable volume" or "a work of great elegance and learning." But Hazlitt's own statement here is that a genuine criticism should "reflect the colours, the light and shade, the soul and body of a work," a sufficiently impressionistic aim perhaps. Most important is his emphasis here once more upon the necessity of judging works according to their own kind, instead of ranging them all in a single order of excellence. There are, he grants, orders of excellence: some subjects are greater than others,[175] and it is not true, as he interprets a remark of Byron's to indicate that it is, that execution is everything and the subject nothing. But Murillo's "Two Beggar Boys," with its commonplace subject, is superior to all but the most finely conceived and executed paintings of great and noble subjects.

One of the chief requirements of the critic, then, is catholicity of taste. Some persons like a simple style, some an ornate: their taste *is* a taste, and is not to be described as right or wrong. There are different kinds, as well as different degrees, of excellence, just as there are different kinds of persons. But the best critic is able to appreciate all these varied excellences, without being under the necessity of subordinating one to another or of crying up one at the expense of another. For this reason Hazlitt has "sometimes thought that the most acute and original-minded men made bad critics," for they see everything too much through a particular medium. In this he was probably thinking of the narrowness of many of Wordsworth's literary judgements, and possibly of Coleridge's intolerance of Dryden and Pope.

Hazlitt, then, as far as he can be classified at all in this

---

[175] This point is discussed more fully in the account of Hazlitt's theory of Taste, from which the problems of criticism and the function of the critic cannot, of course, be separated.—See p. 78 ff., above.

respect, is most nearly at one with the school of "Taste." His reason, once more, is that "systems and opinions change, but nature is always true": [176] that final or absolute knowledge of truth is impossible for us, and that therefore all we can be certain of is our own impressions.

[176] *Lectures on the English Comic Writers,* V. *Works,* VIII, 99.

CONCLUSION

THE primary purpose of the foregoing discussion has
been a purely expository one. It has been felt that if
a re-appraisement of Hazlitt's position as a critic is ever to
be made it must be based upon a knowledge of the broader
aspects of his work which have here been under consideration. This knowledge is not easy to secure. Scattered as it
is, Hazlitt's philosophy and philosophical criticism if
brought together would in mere bulk loom rather formi-
dably. The task of presenting its main features in brief
compass has been rendered more difficult by two other
factors. One is the fact that Hazlitt so early abandoned all
idea of constructing or expounding a systematic philosophy, and that in consequence all his writing except the
Principles of Human Action is more or less occasional or
(from a systematic point of view) fragmentary. The second
is a more serious difficulty—is, indeed, probably the cause
of the first. It is the fact that Hazlitt was essentially a critic
—which means that his ideas came to him, or at least were
formulated, most often as a reaction to something else.
Hence he approached the same subject often from totally
different angles, and often his negative rather than his
positive ideas are the things that stand out upon a first
reading. Yet the positive ideas are there, and are what
entitle him to be considered a philosophical critic. As his
Principles of Human Action grew out of his opposition
to the materialists, so his theory of the *ideal* is expressed
as a criticism of Reynolds, and his explanation of the
function of metre arises from dissatisfaction with Words-

worth's theory. Yet in each of these cases he has constructive ideas not derived from his opponent and often derived from no one but himself. It has been necessary, in order to present a coherent picture of Hazlitt's thought, to take these various ideas from their contexts, and to analyze their relationships with each other, an undertaking which is rendered difficult by Hazlitt's habit of approaching each subject on the grounds and in the terminology of its own school of thought.

The first thing that stands out from a study of the theoretical side of Hazlitt's writing is that he was a philosophical thinker in his own right, and that he would have been this—though not an historically important one—even had he never written a word of literary criticism. Of no other great English critic, perhaps, except Coleridge can this be said. Dryden and Johnson were both frequently involved in theoretical controversies relating to literature, Dryden in his differences with Shadwell and Rymer, for example, Johnson in numerous instances, perhaps most notably in his pronouncement upon the *unities*.[1] But neither one was a philosopher in any sense of the word, or a student of philosophy. Nor was Addison a philosopher, except as we may say that he popularized a certain practical philosophy of life. Pope can hardly claim to rank among the great as a critic, and certainly not as a philosopher. As Johnson said of Pope's one claim to "metaphysical" distinction, the *Essay on Man*, what was true in it was not new, and what was new was not true. Burke and Reynolds indeed have their importance in the development of English æsthetic theory, but then neither of these was a literary

---

[1] In the opinion of Professor Nichol Smith it was Johnson, and not Coleridge or Schlegel, who once for all settled the problem of the dramatic unities.—D. Nichol Smith, *Shakespeare in the Eighteenth Century*, pp. 71–75.

critic. Among Hazlitt's own contemporaries Lamb disliked philosophy as much as he did politics; and De Quincey, though a follower of Coleridge and a self-styled interpreter of Kant was in no sense himself a philosophical
thinker, nor did the subject of philosophy play any important part in his writings. Carlyle is an exception, if
we are to regard him as one of the great critics. His position as a literary critic is a point, however, which we cannot settle here further than to say that, though there is a
good deal of criticism in Carlyle's earlier *Essays*, some of
it perhaps even great criticism, his interest in literature
qua literature was soon so thoroughly eclipsed by devotion to his messages that it ceased to have an independent
existence. And in any case, if we do consider Carlyle one
of the great critics, his philosophy, though more learned
perhaps and more modern in its use of post-Kantian ideas
than Hazlitt's, did not, as Hazlitt's philosophical study
did, work in furtherance of the disinterested criticism of
literature, but rather in opposition to it. His preoccupation with the ethical import of his philosophy, that is,
was actively destructive of the true literary critic's attitude
to his subject in almost precisely the same way as Hazlitt's
philosophy was constructive for his critical attitude. And
again, neither Arnold, nor Ruskin, nor Pater can be said
to have been philosophical thinkers in the sense that
Hazlitt was. Arnold was indeed acquainted in some degree
with German transcendentalism, and he wrote much upon
religion and faith. But there was no speculation in him.
Ruskin's theories of art have, of course, had great influence, and they may perhaps be said to pay their respects
to philosophy through religion. But he was no philosophical thinker, nor was he either, in any important sense,
a literary critic. Pater delivered lectures on *Plato and*

Platonism, and he was interested in working out a philosophy, as appears particularly in *Marius the Epicurean.* But it was a *philosophy of life* that he looked for and neither a speculation nor a science—it was therefore an interested and not a disinterested pursuit. His wave of the hand at "metaphysics" as "the art of bewildering oneself methodically," a definition which he quotes approvingly from Michelet, is no mere rhetorical gesture; he meant what he said here in spite of *Marius.* And although one can piece together from scattered passages in his work a fairly coherent theory of art, he discredits and belittles æsthetic theory as part of a critic's equipment. The true critic should ask himself simply: "What is this song or picture, this engaging personality presented in life or in a book, to *me?* What effect does it really produce on me?" The answers to these questions are the facts upon which true criticism is built, its materials. And "he who experiences these impressions strongly, and drives directly at the analysis and discrimination of them, need not trouble himself with the abstract question what beauty is in itself, or its exact relation to truth or experience,— metaphysical questions, as unprofitable as metaphysical questions elsewhere. He may pass them all by as being, answerable or not, of no interest to him." What the critic does need is "a certain kind of temperament, the power of being deeply moved by the presence of beautiful objects" [2]—what, in Hazlitt's day and before, would have been known simply as *sensibility.* As for the minor critics of the Pre-Raphaelite and "art for art's sake" or æsthetic schools, they were, after all, minor, and though they played a good deal upon the fringes of philosophy, they were not themselves philosophical.

[2] See the Preface to *The Renaissance.*

That a background of philosophical knowledge and a power of abstract thought have great value for a critic is what few will deny, particularly when it is coupled with a strong sense of fact, a concreteness of thought, which keeps the critic steadily in touch with the actual objects of his criticism. This latter faculty Hazlitt had, in a far greater degree [3] than Coleridge. And although his philosophical thought was inferior to Coleridge's in grasp, in breadth, and especially in imaginativeness, and was not comparable to it in influence, it must be remembered that it was at least distinctively his own. His philosophy had already taken its special direction and to some extent even its form before he met Coleridge, and although there are many points of contact between them, it remained essentially distinct and even opposed to the thought of Coleridge ever afterward. It is true that as a philosopher Hazlitt might with advantage have been more truly "metaphysical" than he was, and that he might have had a fuller knowledge of the Platonic tradition and of the work of Kant. The whole course of philosophy was altered, its channels were deepened and the problems which it faced were transformed under the influence of the Kantian philosophy. The same was true, though in a much less radical sense, in the field of æsthetics in consequence of the work of Lessing. To have been ignorant of the work of these two men was, if not a fault, certainly a serious disadvantage. It was enough perhaps to prevent any philosophical writer from exerting much influence upon his contemporaries or upon his successors for several generations. Certainly it was enough to make some of Hazlitt's writing seem far more "dated" than does that of his greatest contemporaries. Yet this is not the whole

[3] Some persons would say, to his disadvantage.

story of Hazlitt's philosophy. For it is beginning to appear now in the light of modern thought, that the great writers who erected the nineteenth-century philosophy of Idealism upon Kant's foundations attempted their synthesis too soon or too hastily; and we are having to turn back and pick up the lost thread—which we call, roughly, realism—not quite at the point where Kant found it in eighteenth-century philosophy, but perhaps at the point where he left it. It is in picking up this line of thought once more that we meet Hazlitt.

Some of Hazlitt's arguments against the empiricists, however ingenious, are little more than quaint to us now. But his fundamental philosophical attitude is by no means quaint; indeed it is more in tune with the best of modern realistic thought than it has been with any other school in the past. Modern philosophy is faced with a new science and a new psychology. If it is to succeed in achieving a synthesis satisfactory to our age, it must find a place for both. Hazlitt had nothing to say on the side of science. But in philosophical psychology the ground of his disagreement with the eighteenth-century empiricists and utilitarians, and of his difference from Rousseau is almost precisely, though often phrased in antiquated terms, the same as that of modern thought. For much modern psychology goes back to the eighteenth century, "with a difference," and Hazlitt too wore his empiricism with a difference. His insistence upon *feeling* as the mainspring of human action, without either idealizing emotion or making it an end in itself as Rousseau did, and at the same time without translating it into the narrow channel of simple self-preservation as the utilitarians did—this has come to be one of the most important postulates of the best psychological thought of today.

Hazlitt's pluralism too is in many respects modern. Though a strict pluralism will probably never be a fashionable philosophy, yet the recognition which it involves of man's tendency to see what is manifold as one, because of the constitution of his own mind rather than because of oneness in the phenomenon—is essential both to modern science and to modern psychology.

Finally, whether the reader be a realist (in the broader sense of the word), or an idealist and therefore unwilling to admit anything of ultimate philosophical value in Hazlitt's point of view, he cannot, I think, question the value of such a viewpoint for a literary critic. It is in this that Hazlitt's work maintains, in spite of certain superficial contradictions, an essential unity throughout. It may even be said that his philosophy, his critical principles, and his concrete criticism present a greater unity than do those of any other great English critic. In speaking of Dryden and Johnson, for example, we are accustomed to consider their critical canons as, on the whole and with certain exceptions, false, to dismiss them as inheritances largely from the French; and then to emphasize the critics' sound sense and judgement as it operates on the actual material for criticism. As for Arnold, we may accept many of his canons of criticism, and must certainly admire their fitness for the situation of his own day. But we are constantly having to admit that he rode his theories too hard in the application and so came to grief often in specific cases. It is an indication of how far we have become accustomed to the necessity of separating a writer's theory or philosophy from his practice in criticism, that even so thoughtful a person as Mr. Shawcross seems aware of nothing unusual in his attitude toward Coleridge in this respect. Mr. Shawcross objects to Coleridge's contemporaries in criticism on the ground of their having no laws or canons since "classical" tradition had been overthrown; whereas Coleridge, he believes, gave us "a truly critical criticism"—that is, a criticism based on general principles.[4] Yet in a previous passage Mr. Shawcross had said: "It is true that Coleridge himself makes no direct application of the conclusions at which he had arrived"; and he explains in a note that this failure arises no doubt partly from "the difficulty, if not impossibility, of applying philosophical theories of art to the criticism of any particular work of art—a fact to which Schiller draws attention . . ." The "poetical criticism" of the second part of the *Biographia Literaria* is based, he says, "not on the deductions of the metaphysician, but on the intuitive insight of the poet." [5] We expect, of course, to find in all departments of life some difference between theory and practice. But to go as far as does Mr. Shawcross here, is to make us question the value or the truth of a theory of art which cannot be applied to particular works.

Hazlitt, when he sat down to criticize a book or play, or a picture, did not indeed ask himself what rules and laws it followed or failed to follow. In fact, for this kind of "foot-rule" criticism he had the greatest scorn; criticism was not to be like laying out the specifications for a building. But his philosophy was very much a part of himself, and one of its main tenets was that truth is not one but many. So he was always looking for truth and had no preconceptions against it when he met it. And again what I have called his "projectivism"—his belief that the dualism of self and other, or the satisfaction of the desire for knowledge, is to be achieved by "going out of the

[4] *Op. cit.*, p. lxxxviii.
[5] *Ibid.*, pp. lxxv–lxxvi.

self to others" instead of taking in all things—this is precisely in a generalized form a statement of one of his greatest virtues as a critic. These philosophical tenets come out in his criticism as an impartial catholicity of taste and a remarkable power of identifying himself intensely with the greatest variety of persons and situations. Like Keats, who once wrote that when he looked out of his window at a sparrow on the gravel he *was* that sparrow, scratching and pecking at food—so Hazlitt when he thought of Clarissa became Clarissa herself, or became that strange little person Richardson, alone in his study contemplating the Idea of his divine Clarissa. It was an identifying power that could often overcome even his deepest prejudices. There was nothing that Hazlitt hated so much as "legitimacy" and the Bourbons. Yet in writing of French plays he is quite willing to experience their charm and that of the court of Louis XIV: "Happy time! Enviable time to think of! When vanity and folly expanded in full bloom, and were spread out ostentatiously like the figures in a gaudy tapestry instead of being folded up and thrust into a corner by the hand of a cynic and austere philosophy." [6] Here irony and sympathy are mingled, but the sympathy is there.

Hazlitt's theory of the *ideal,* whether in literature or the fine arts, shows again how the same foundation underlies his thought. The *ideal* is not to draw all things to oneself or to a single self-created idea; it is not the average of all forms, it is not simplification; the *ideal* is manifold, each its own kind, to be found in an infinite number of extremes and not in one mean. It is, instead, the *ideal* of a pluralistic philosophy. And this, it may be noted in passing, allows Hazlitt to find a place in art for the

[6] "French Plays," *Works,* XI, 354.

grotesque, which has not always been easy to fit into other systems.

Finally, Hazlitt's philosophy of *feeling* saved him from certain very likely sources of error in his concrete criticism. In the first place it saved him from the arid intellectualism that early familiarity with neo-classical literature and materialistic philosophy might conceivably have developed. But it saved him also from the literal and carping spirit of a certain sort of realist. He never failed, that is, to take into account the imponderables of life, never was led away by the supposition that to "count the button-holes" of an Indian chief was to portray the chief. A recognition of the importance of feeling in human life is at once an opening wedge to imagination. On the other hand, as we have already indicated, Hazlitt never fell into sentimentalism, as the philosopher of *feeling* in Rousseau's sense is almost bound to do.

Hazlitt, then, stands as one of the earliest of modern realists, in the best sense of that term. Indeed, one might with reasonable assurance say that he is the only consistent realist among the great English critics. For although Dryden and Johnson were realistic in temperament, they were hampered by the formalism of critical canons in which their common sense very often did not concur. This was not the case with Hazlitt: such beliefs as he held were actually applicable to literature and art. His basic soundness is sometimes obscured for the reader by the fact that, in theoretical discussions of painting especially, he is so intent upon counteracting the influence of Reynolds and the older theorists who insisted upon generalizing and "improving" nature, that he often re-iterates only that the artist must "imitate nature," not stopping to qualify or explain further. Hence the casual reader may at times suppose that all Hazlitt advocated in theory was a very literal fidelity to external fact.[7] But often enough he explained this imitation as involving the state of mind, the sympathy, and the purpose of the artist, and thereby showed how well he knew that the *truth* and *nature* upon which the artist works are within himself as well as without.

This realistic philosophy of Hazlitt's, with its influence upon his critical work, places him in a position in relation to the development of English criticism which has never been recognized. Because it has been assumed that his general ideas, so far as he had any, were Coleridge's, he has to a considerable degree been misplaced in critical history, has been simply grouped, with very little differentiation from them, with Lamb, Coleridge, De Quincey, Hunt, Landor (with reservations), as among those who reproduced and interpreted in prose the romanticism, or the various romanticisms, as some prefer to consider it, already established in poetry. But he actually holds, or should hold, a quite separate position and one of greater importance because it is both unique among English critics and valuable in itself—the position, that is, of showing how with a reasoned philosophy behind him the non-mystical, non-transcendental, the non-didactic, even the sceptical man may find significant values in literature and art without descending to what always seems the lower plane of most hedonistic thought. Hazlitt's is a funda-

[7] Even Professor Chase sees this as the sum of Hazlitt's theory of art, and concludes, in consequence, that Hazlitt was a realist in theory and a romanticist in judging individual works. Here, however, Professor Chase fails to take into account all that Hazlitt meant by "imitation of nature," and fails to see also how his philosophy of feeling unifies what Professor Chase calls his realism and his romanticism (using the former term in a narrower and more unfavorable sense than that in which I have taken it).

mental philosophic attitude which, had it been maintained and developed afterward in the same vital relation
to literature that it had in his work, might in our own
day have furnished another alternative than Anglo-
Catholicism for such disillusioned æsthetes as Mr. T. S.
Eliot.

But in more specific and less hypothetical ways than this
Hazlitt has also made his contribution. His theory of perception with its modifications of Hartley's associationism,
though it is very similar to Coleridge's idea at bottom, is
brought by Hazlitt for the first time into a significant relation with painting and literature (while Coleridge
applied it to science). His insistence upon the fact that
interest or passion, mood or character play their part, as
well as does the perceived object, in every act of perception, is carried over into his account of the selectiveness
of the artist and the subjectivity of his vision. And closely
related to his theory of perception is his favorite doctrine
of abstract ideas as resulting from the limitation rather
than from the greatness of the human mind, from our
tendency to make all things simple in order to comprehend them. This, despite some confusion of terms, provides an interesting philosophical foundation for his
insistent belief in concreteness and individuality in art,
a belief which other romantic critics held usually without
any rational explanation. Hazlitt's theory, although not
every one perhaps would accept it, does provide at least
as satisfactorily as any other that has been devised, an
explanation of the æsthetic quality common to both art
and pure science, despite the in other respects antithetic
character of the two pursuits.

In the field of criticism proper Hazlitt has a far greater
and finer body of general ideas than has hitherto been

recognized, and again, as in his philosophical writing, they are on the whole his own ideas and not Coleridge's. They differ from the critical pronouncements of Arnold from many of those of Coleridge, and from most of the earlier critical dicta, however, in being analytical rather than didactic—and perhaps they are none the worse or less enlightening for that. He tells us, for example, not so much what poetry *should be* as what poetry *is*. Perhaps his two most valuable contributions in this kind of general criticism are his account of the function of metre in poetry and his discussion of didactic literature. As we have already seen, none of his contemporaries gave as subtle and at the same time as psychologically accurate an account of the *raison d'être* of metre as Hazlitt did.

In his idea of the relation of literature to morality Hazlitt is probably the soundest critic we have. On this point he not only analyzes but also lays down the law. He does not fall into the error of the "art for art's sake" critics of a later date, who divorced literature from life and therefore also from morality. Yet he frees himself altogether from the long bondage of the idea that art was meant for "instruction and delight." The ramifications of theory and the alternations of emphasis upon one or the other of these ends of poetry in seventeenth- and eighteenth-century criticism are not for us to trace here. In the next age both Coleridge and Wordsworth stated in unmistakable terms their conviction that to give pleasure is the proper end of poetry. Coleridge defines poetry as "the excitement of emotion for the purpose of immediate pleasure, through the medium of beauty." [8] Wordsworth says that "the end of Poetry is to produce excitement in

[8] *On the Principles of Sound Criticism concerning the Fine Arts,* Essay Second, *Miscellanies, Æsthetic and Literary,* p. 10.

coexistence with an overbalance of pleasure."[9] But by neither is the principle maintained consistently. Wordsworth departs from it to some extent at least in his practice. Coleridge has no sooner enunciated the principle than he begins to modify it. Often he deserts it completely —even in his earlier years—as is shown by his plan, already cited,[10] to write an essay on poetry which shall in reality be, as he says, "a disguised system of morals and politics." Hazlitt is the first important writer to assert and maintain with almost complete consistency both in his theory and in his concrete criticism that to give pleasure is the true aim of art. Often enough the reader or beholder receives "instruction," learns something that he did not know; but this very increase of knowledge is itself a pleasure, and only insofar as it is so are we justified in calling it art. "To embody an abstract theory, as if it were a given part of actual nature is an impertinence and indecorum"; that is, to borrow the authority of "nature" for the purpose of proving our own point or moral, is to subvert the truth. Therefore drama (or fiction or poetry) is most moral when it presents "the truest and most intelligible picture of life."[11] It is the soundness of this attitude toward art that has made Hazlitt's criticism of Restoration comedy perhaps the best that has ever been written. Certainly his approach to it is the only one justifiable for the true critic. As Professor Shelly says: "His is the only criticism of these plays that I know of that is not spoiled by what Lamb might call 'the sophisticating medium of moral uses.'" Even Lamb's defense of Restoration comedy, for all its charm, is founded upon a

[9] Preface to Second Edition of the *Lyrical Ballads*.
[10] P. 152, above.
[11] Cf. p. 150 ff., above.

misconception of actual history. In saying that we need not think these comedies immoral because they represent an unreal world in which morals do not exist he is farther from the truth than is Hazlitt who accepts them as founded upon the current life of their day and who proceeds to criticize them as plays, and not to castigate their characters or authors for being what they were.[12] It is not true, as Lamb appears to imply, that Restoration comedy was a species of fairy tale.

Less important than his view of the morals of literature, yet still of value, is Hazlitt's distinction, the origin of which has always been attributed to De Quincey, between science and art: "the one is knowledge—the other power." Like almost all Hazlitt's pronouncements, this is not a chance hit of the intuitive faculty happily directed, but a natural outgrowth of his whole attitude toward life as indicated both in his philosophy and in his concrete criticism. The idea is therefore developed here and there throughout his work in many illuminating ways.

We have been concerned throughout our discussion with only one aspect of Hazlitt's criticism, but it is an aspect which has been altogether neglected in the past. Hazlitt himself, to be sure, is responsible for this neglect. The very excellence of his concrete criticism, its brilliance of phrase, its depth of insight, have so overshadowed the other side of his critical work that we find ourselves in the situation of one who cannot see the sky for the stars. Hazlitt stands in his own light in another way too. There was a certain modesty in him which prevented his ever looking upon himself as a prophet to his age, and which would have prevented this even had his philosophy of art

[12] Shelly, *op. cit.*, p. xxviii; and Bonamy Dobrée, *Restoration Comedy*, pp. 23 and 121.

been of much farther-reaching importance than it was. A man's opinion of himself does in part determine what others think of him, and Hazlitt was always conscious of his deficiencies. In this he stands in contrast to Coleridge, who sometimes conceived himself about to unite for all time in a single universal system art, philosophy, morality, and the Church of England, and who always looked upon himself as the great teacher of his countrymen. Matthew Arnold too, at a later date, saw himself as the enlightened prophet come with a message to mankind; he delivered his critical canons accordingly with the weight of pontifical authority. But Hazlitt did not. He said what he thought, and had done with it.

On the ground of theory alone Hazlitt would not have been a very great critic or philosopher. The account that has been given here shows neither a complete system of art theory constructed, nor many truths discovered that were both new and important. But it does, I hope, serve to show that there was a really respectable body of theory, a group of underlying principles in Hazlitt's criticism which served to bind together his diverse work into a comprehensible whole; and that among great English critics a few of these principles were unique. It is partly because these theoretical aspects of Hazlitt's work have not hitherto received attention that the attitude of later writers toward him has been on the whole one of condescension. As a critic he has been considered a very fine describer of other men's good things, and that is all. But Hazlitt was more than this; he was a critic with a philosophy of his own, and possessed of a theory of art that did much to broaden his taste and deepen and strengthen his judgements. The experience which any modern reader has, in dipping into Hazlitt, of finding himself startled here and there by a remark which, it would seem, must have been written only yesterday—this is no accident, no mere chance of brilliant intuition. It is the result of a fundamentally modern philosophy of life and art, of a realism so broad as to include not only the visible universe but the invisible world of thought and feeling as well.

Appendix

HAZLITT'S READING

IT has been generally said that Hazlitt's criticism suffers from a lack of that breadth of knowledge and reading which has been one of the resources of other great critics. Certainly Hazlitt was nothing like the reader that Coleridge or De Quincey was. His ignorance has, however, been greatly exaggerated. Saintsbury, from the conscious height of his own voracious appetite for print, considers this lack of knowledge the most obvious fault in Hazlitt as a critic. "Would all men were as honest!" he remarks, "but one cannot say, 'Would all critics were as ignorant!' " [1] And further, in discussing the lack of familiarity with foreign literature among the romantic critics as a whole, he says that even Coleridge and De Quincey were "very imperfectly" acquainted with French literature, that Leigh Hunt knew little but Italian (and not the most important work in that language), but that "Hazlitt's case is worse still, for he evidently knew very little indeed, either of the classics or of foreign modern literature, except a few philosophic writers, here of next to no use. In fact, one cannot help wondering how, knowing so little, he came to judge so well—till the wonder nearly disappears, as we see how much better he would have judged if he had known more." [2] Hazlitt, however, had already published his answer to Saintsbury on this point: "To a want of general reading, I plead guilty, and

[1] *Op. cit.*, III, 252.
[2] *Ibid.*, pp. 412–413.—Professor Nichol Smith in the introduction to *Hazlitt: Essays on Poetry* says that Hazlitt "knew no foreign influence." But the influence of French literature and philosophy upon him was considerable, as has been seen.

am sorry for it; but perhaps if I had read more, I might have thought less." [3]

Hazlitt himself is partly responsible for the exaggerated picture of his ignorance that has come down to us: the standard by which he measured himself seems always to have been that of Coleridge's vast reading. When he admits to knowing little of Aristophanes and Lucian, we not only take him at his word, but are inclined to assume that he had read nothing of either —which was not the case. We recall Procter's account of how, having engaged to give a course of lectures on the Elizabethan drama, Hazlitt borrowed from him "about a dozen volumes, comprehending the finest of the old plays," retired to Winterslow, and returned in six weeks with the subject mastered and the lectures written.[4] The fact of this is not altered, though the impression is, when we read Hazlitt's remark, published in the following year, that he has read "only a dozen or fourteen" of the plays of Beaumont and Fletcher, though he means sometime to read the rest.[5] For a modern Elizabethan scholar a dozen plays of Beaumont and Fletcher is not much; but for a lecturer in 1820 it was not little.

Hazlitt's acquaintance with foreign languages was assuredly slight; but it was not quite as negligible as Saintsbury implies. It is therefore well to realize just how extensive it was. Hazlitt knew and read Latin, though his familiarity with Latin literature was very limited.[6] He had studied some Greek, but it is unlikely that he could read it well. He never quotes from any

---

[3] "On the Causes of Popular Opinion." *Works*, XII, 320.

[4] Howe, *Life*, pp. 279–280.

[5] The lectures were delivered in 1820. This statement occurs in the essay "On Reading Old Books," which was first published in February, 1821.—*Works*, VII, 229 and 499.

[6] He quoted constantly from Horace's *Ars Poetica*, in Latin; he spoke familiarly of Cicero's Latin style and occasionally of other writers. His early studies in the language are described in his letters to his father from Hackney, which are quoted in part in the first chapter of Howe's *Life*, and in full by W. C. Hazlitt in the *Memoirs*, [Vol. I, Bk. I., Chapters I and II.]. From these it is at least clear that he was reading Ovid at the age of ten. He also studied Hebrew at Hackney.

Greek writers in the original.[7] The study of French he began
as a child; and he was familiar with the language before his
first visit to Paris in 1802, although for a short time after his
arrival he found himself somewhat "perplexed" in conversation.[8] Of French literature he knew far more than "a few
philosophic writers." His interest in the French theatre was
great, and he knew its classical dramatists well, though he was
more than a little critical of them. From Rabelais and Montaigne, through Rousseau, to his friend Stendhal his familiarity
with standard French literature in the original was far more
extensive than that of almost any of his romantic contemporaries. On the other hand, he suffered, in comparison with some
of his contemporaries, from a lack of acquaintance with the
German language. He seems to have undertaken to learn
Italian some five years before his death.[9]

These things do not make of Hazlitt a learned man. But the
superstition of his being conspicuously ignorant should be dis-
missed. For this reason, as well as for reasons stated in the *Introduction*,[10] a list of the books Hazlitt is known to have read
in the field covered by the present study is added here. Much
that Hazlitt read, on these subjects as well as on others, we
cannot trace with certainty, partly because, as has already
been said,[11] the period of his greatest reading—the years before
about 1805—preceded his years of writing, so that his essays
are not full of references to his current reading as they might
otherwise have been. Many things that Hazlitt probably read,

[7] For such evidence as exists regarding his knowledge of Greek, see
W. C. Hazlitt, *The Hazlitts*, I, 399, and 405–406; the *Reply to Z*, p. 36; the
Letter to William Gifford, Esq., Works, I, 401.

[8] W. C. Hazlitt, *Memoirs of William Hazlitt*, I, 86.

[9] "I bought a little Florentine edition of Petrarch and Dante the other
day, and have made out one page," he writes in a letter to Landor (1825).
—Howe, *Life*, p. 379.—Hazlitt's son says that he and his father translated
from the Italian Ticozzi's life of Titian, which they published in 1830
with Northcote's *Life of Titian*.—Howe, *Life*, p. 411 n. and W. Hazlitt,
Literary Remains, p. lxvi.

[10] Pp. 2–3.

[11] P. 7, above.

some even that he almost certainly knew, are therefore omitted from the list for lack of conclusive evidence. Nothing of Diderot's appears,[12] for reasons that have already been given, although the probability is very strong that Hazlitt had read at least Diderot's *Essai sur la Peinture* and although it is generally taken for granted that he had read all the Encyclopædists in his youth. Voltaire's name does not occur in the list, for though in a number of passages Hazlitt refers familiarly to the work and opinions of the Frenchman, it is not possible to be certain just which works (with the exception of *Candide*) he had read. The same thing is true of Chateaubriand, some of whose writing Hazlitt certainly knew. In many other cases—notably with Plato's *Republic*, Aristotle's *Poetics* and *Metaphysics*, Longinus, Spinoza, Malebranche—Hazlitt speaks quite definitely of their content; yet in all these cases one cannot be sure that he is not writing from second-hand knowledge.

Certain other works have been omitted from the list for another reason. Hazlitt was thoroughly familiar with the criticism of the major English writers of the preceding age. He knew Dryden's prefaces as well as his plays and poetry; he knew Pope thoroughly, and Dr. Johnson and Goldsmith. He was familiar with the criticism that had appeared in the *Tatler* and the *Spectator*. At the same time, his familiarity with these writers is so habitual that he often fails to make his references to their work very precise. Any partial list of Hazlitt's reading of their work, based upon definite references that can be identified, as the rest of the list is, would be so incomplete as to be totally misleading. It has therefore been thought best to omit Dryden, Pope, Johnson, and Goldsmith altogether. Of contemporary writers, Hazlitt read all that Coleridge, Wordsworth, Lamb, and Leigh Hunt published during his lifetime, and most of the writing of Southey. The separate critical works of these have not been listed.

A word, however, must be said of the principles upon which

[12] Except his contributions to Baron Grimm's *Correspondances*. See p. 55, above.

works have been admitted to the list. A mere quotation or two on the part of Hazlitt, particularly of a striking phrase, is no evidence of his having read the work from which it came. He introduces as a quotation, for example, the remark that "to imitate the Iliad is not to imitate Homer," which, in slightly different words, comes from Edward Young's *Conjectures on Original Composition*.[13] But the remark is quoted by Reynolds in his *Discourses*, where Hazlitt may have seen it, and is in any case such a remark as one might pick up anywhere. And again, Hazlitt uses a phrase, "the butt and the wit, the jester and the jest," which is a telescoped quotation from Maurice Morgann's *Essay on the Dramatic Character of Falstaff*. Mr. P. L. Carver in the *Review of English Studies* (July, 1930) and Mr. Howe in the notes to his edition of Hazlitt (XVI, 429) suppose that Hazlitt had read Morgann's *Essay*. It is very likely that he had, but again precise evidence is lacking, and Morgann's *Essay* is not included in this list. Many of the titles included are of books which Hazlitt explicitly states that he has read, or from which he quotes with page references. Nearly all the rest are works which we can be sure that he knew at first hand, either from clear implications in his way of speaking of them (Hazlitt is never deliberately deceptive in this respect) or from his close familiarity with their content. A very few titles have been introduced on other evidence such as a reference to having procured a book for Hazlitt in a letter to him from Lamb, or a statement by William Carew Hazlitt that he possessed a book of his grandfather's.

We should perhaps know more of Hazlitt's reading if he had owned more books. But he never had many, and certainly some that he did possess must have perished from time to time, like the lost fragments of his lectures on philosophy which had grown undecipherable in an old hamper in a lodging-house cellar. A few of his books came into the possession of his grandson, William Carew Hazlitt; but even these have not been

---

[13] This quotation is not identified by Waller and Glover.

traceable since the latter's death, and no list of them seems to have been preserved.

In preparation of the following list the aid afforded by the excellent notes to the Waller and Glover edition of Hazlitt's Works has been invaluable. Mr. Howe's additional notes, in those volumes of his edition which have appeared, have also been of very great service.

Hazlitt's Reading in Philosophy, Æsthetics, and Criticism.

Francis Bacon. *Advancement of Learning.*
————. *De Sapientia Veterum* (probably in translation)
————. *Essays.*
————. *Novum Organum.*
James Barry. *Letter to the Dilettanti Society.*
————. *Works.*
Richard Bentley. *Boyle Lectures.*
George Berkeley. *Essay towards a New Theory of Vision.*
————. *Alciphron, or the Minute Philosopher.*
————. *A Treatise concerning the Principles of Human Knowledge.*
Nicolas Boileau. *Satires.*
Etienne Bonnot de Condillac. *La Logique.*
(Sir) Thomas Browne. *Religio Medici.*
Edmund Burke. *Essay on the Sublime and Beautiful.*
Joseph Butler. *The Analogy of Religion, Natural and Revealed, to the Constitution and Course of Nature.*
————. *Fifteen Sermons Preached at the Rolls Chapel.*
Lord Byron. *Letter to [John Murray] "On the Rev. Wm. L. Bowles's Strictures on the Life and Writings of Pope."*
George Campbell. *Philosophy of Rhetoric.*
Benvenuto Cellini. *Autobiography.*
Thomas Chalmers. *Discourses on the Christian Revelation, viewed in connection with Modern Astronomy.*
William Ellery Channing. *Sermons and Tracts: including Re-*

marks on the Character and Writings of Milton, and of
Fenelon. . . .

Thomas Chubb. *Tracts.*

——————. *Posthumous Works.*

Colley Cibber. *Apology for his Life.*

Samuel Clarke. *A Demonstration of the Being and Attributes
of God.*

William Collins. *Epistle to Sir Thomas Hanmer.*

——————. *Ode on the Poetical Character.*

Condillac. *See* Bonnot.

Thomas Cooper ("of Manchester"). *"Essays."* (so called by Hazlitt. Perhaps his *Tracts, Ethical, Theological and Political*).

Charles Antoine Coypel. *Discourses on Art.*

Hector St. John Crèvecoeur. *Letters from an American Farmer.*

John Dennis. *Remarks upon Cato.*

Destutt de Tracy. *Elémens d'Idéologie.*

Diderot. *See* Grimm.

(Sir) Kenelm Digby. *Observations upon Religio Medici.*

Jonathan Edwards. *Enquiry into the* . . . *Freedom of Will.*

Joseph Farington. *Memoirs of the Life of Sir Joshua Reynolds.*

George Farquhar. *"Letters"* (probably in one of the many
eighteenth-century editions of his works which contained
"all his poems, letters," etc.).

John Fearn. *Essay on Consciousness.*

John Flaxman. *Lectures on Sculpture.* . . . *As delivered before the* . . . *Royal Academy.*

Henry Fuseli. *Lectures on Painting, delivered at the Royal
Academy.*

William Godwin. *Enquiry concerning Political Justice.*

Thomas Gray. *Letters.*

Maria Graham (Lady Callcott). *Memoirs of the Life of Nicho-
las Poussin.*

Frederic Melchior, Baron de Grimm. *Mémoires Historiques,
Littéraires et Anecdotiques.*[14]

14 It may have been an abridgment, in four volumes, of this work that

James Harris. *Hermes, or a Philosophical Inquiry concerning Universal Grammar.*

David Hartley. *Observations on Man.*

Claude Adrien Helvétius. *De l'Esprit.*

Thomas Herring. *Letters to William Duncombe, Esq., 1728–1757.*

Thomas Hobbes. *Behemoth.*

————. *Leviathan.*

————. *Tripos.* (Hazlitt had read this, including its three parts to which he refers, and which were sometimes published, as separate works: the *Discourse of Human Nature,* the *De Corpore Politico,* and *Liberty and Necessity.*)

D'Holbach (Paul Henri Thiry). *Système de la Nature.*

Henry Home (Lord Kames). *Sketches of the History of Man.*

Horace. *Ars Poetica.*[15]

David Hume. *A Treatise of Human Nature.*

————. *Essays.*

Kames. See Home.

Kant. See Willich.

John Kemble. *Macbeth and King Richard III, an answer to* [Whately's] *Remarks.*

John Locke. *An Essay concerning Human Understanding.*

(Sir) James Mackintosh. Lectures on *The Law of Nature and Nations.*[16]

Edmund Malone. Hazlitt at least part of the time used Malone's edition of Shakespeare.[17]

Bernard de Mandeville. *Fable of the Bees.*

Hazlitt read. He probably saw also the two volumes of it in English brought out by Colburn in 1814. In one passage concerning the *Correspondances* Hazlitt gives a page reference. This corresponds neither to that of the eleven volumes published in Paris (Buisson) in 1812–1813, nor to that of Colburn's English abridgment. The reference probably is to the larger French abridgment, though I have not been able to check this.

15 See also Roscommon.

16 Hazlitt heard these lectures.

17 For a full account of the question of the text of Shakespeare used by Hazlitt, see Howe's edition of Hazlitt's works, v. IV, 391.

William Melmoth. *Fitzosborne's Letters.*

Anthony Raphael Mengs. *Works.*

Lady Mary Wortley Montague. *Letters.*

Michel de Montaigne. *Essais.*

Charles de St. Bavon de Montesquieu. *Esprit des Lois.*

James Northcote. *Memoirs of Sir Joshua Reynolds.*

John Opie. *Lectures on Painting delivered at the Royal Academy.*

William Paley. *Moral and Political Philosophy.*

————. *Evidences of Christianity.*

Joseph Priestley. *The Doctrine of Philosophical Necessity Illustrated.*

————. *Letters to a Philosophical Unbeliever.*

Thomas Reid. *Inquiry into the Human Mind.*

Sir Joshua Reynolds. *Discourses on Art.*

————. *Three Letters to the Idler.*

————. *See also* Farington *and* Northcote.

Jonathan Richardson. *Essays.*

————. *On the Science of a Connoisseur.*

————. *Theory of Painting.*

William Richardson. *Essays on Shakespeare's Dramatic Characters.*

François Duc de La Rochefoucauld. *Maxims.*

Wentworth Dillon, Earl of Roscommon. *Horace's Art of Poetry* [translation into English verse].

Jean Jacques Rousseau. *Confessions.*

————. *Discours sur l'Origine et les Fondements de l'Inégalité parmi les Hommes.*

————. *Emile.*

————. *Lettre à D'Alembert.*

————. *The New Eloise.*[18]

————. *Reveries of a Solitary Walker.*[18]

[18] English title indicates that Hazlitt probably read these in translation, though he may have been familiar with them in the original as with the others.

————. "Dedication to the Social Contract with other pieces of Rousseau." [19]

August Wilhelm von Schlegel. *Lectures on Dramatic Art and Literature* [translation by John Black].

Shaftesbury. *Characteristics.*

William Shenstone. *Letters.* (so called by Hazlitt. Perhaps *Recollection of Some Particulars in the Life of* . . . *William Shenstone, in a series of Letters.* . . .)

Jean C. L. S. de Sismondi. *Histoire des Republiques Italiennes du Moyen-Age.*

————. *Littérature du Midi de l'Europe.*

Adam Smith. *Wealth of Nations.*

————. *Theory of Moral Sentiments.*

Joseph Spence. *Anecdotes, Observations, and Characters of Books and Men.*

Madame de Staël. *De l'Allemagne.*

————. *Lettres sur J. J. Rousseau.*

Stendhal. (Marie Henri Beyle). *De l'Amour.*

Dugald Stewart. *Dissertation on the Rise and Progress of Modern Metaphysics.* (Prefixed to Supplement of 4th and 5th editions of the *Encyclopedia Britannica.*)

(Sir) William Temple. *Essays.*

P. F. Tingry. *The Painter and Varnisher's Guide.*

Horne Tooke. *Diversions of Purley.*

Abraham Tucker. *The Light of Nature Pursued.*

James Usher. *An Introduction to the Theory of the Human Mind.*

Giorgio Vasari. *Lives of the Painters.*

Horace Walpole. *Letters.*

Joseph Warton. *An Essay on the Writings and Genius of Pope.*

Thomas Warton. *History of English Poetry.*

---

[19] This is Hazlitt's account of the volume. I have failed to identify it otherwise.

Thomas Whately. *Remarks on Some of the Characters of Shakespeare.*

A. F. M. Willich. *Elements of the Critical Philosophy.*[20]

[20] The title page reads "translated by" Willich, but the work is rather an interpretation than a translation of Kant.

BIBLIOGRAPHY

HAZLITT'S WORKS

Collected Works. ed. Waller and Glover, 12 v. London, 1902–1904. Index, 1906.

New Writings of William Hazlitt, First and Second Series. ed. P. P. Howe. 2 v. London, 1925–1927.

The Complete Works of William Hazlitt, ed. P. P. Howe. Vols. I–XI, XVI–XVII. London, 1930–.

Abridgment of the Light of Nature Pursued, by Abraham Tucker, Esq. London, 1807.

Liber Amoris, or The New Pygmalion. Privately printed, n. pl., 1894.

Life of Napoleon Buonaparte. New York, 1847.

A New and Improved Grammar of the English Tongue . . . London, 1810.

A Reply to Z. With Introduction by Charles Whibley. London, 1923.

Select British Poets, or New Elegant Extracts from Chaucer to the Present Time. London, 1824.

BOOKS, ESSAYS, AND ARTICLES ON HAZLITT

Jules Douady. *Liste Chronologique des Oeuvres de William Hazlitt.* Paris, 1906.

P. P. Howe. *The Life of William Hazlitt.* 3rd ed. London, 1928.

Augustine Birrell. *William Hazlitt.* London, 1902.

William Hazlitt (the son). *Literary Remains of the Late William Hazlitt with a Notice of his Life, by his Son and Thoughts on his Genius and Writings, by E. S. Bulwer and Sergeant Talfourd, etc.* 2 v. London, 1836.

W. C. Hazlitt. *Four Generations of a Literary Family.* 2 v. London, 1897.

——————. *Memoirs of William Hazlitt.* 2 v. London, 1867.

——————. *Lamb and Hazlitt.* London, 1900.

——————. *The Hazlitts: an Account of their Origin and Descent.* Privately printed, n. pl., 1911.

Alexander Ireland. *William Hazlitt, Essayist and Critic.* Selections, with a Memoir. London, 1889.

Leslie Stephen. "*William Hazlitt,*" in II, 290–343, *Hours in a Library.* 3 v. London, 1909.

H. W. Garrod. "The Place of Hazlitt in English Criticism," in *The Profession of Poetry and other Lectures.* Oxford, 1929.

W. P. Ker. "Hazlitt." I, 242–257 in *Collected Essays of William Paton Ker.* 2 v. London, 1925.

C. Madison. "William Hazlitt, Man and Critic" in *Poet Lore,* XL (1929), p. 373 ff.

Virginia Woolf. "William Hazlitt," in *Second Common Reader.* New York, 1932.

Percy V. D. Shelly. *Essays by William Hazlitt.* New York, 1924. Introduction.

D. Nichol Smith. *Hazlitt: Essays on Poetry.* Edinburgh and London, 1906. Introduction.

J. Zeitlin. *Hazlitt on English Literature.* New York, 1913. Introduction.

Edmund Gosse. *Conversations of Northcote by William Hazlitt, with an Essay on Hazlitt as Art Critic.* London, 1894.

Stanley P. Chase. "Hazlitt as a Critic of Art." *Publications of the Modern Language Association.* Vol. 39 (1924). pp. 179–202.

R. W. Babcock. "The Direct Influence of Late Eighteenth Century Shakespeare Criticism on Hazlitt and Coleridge," in *Modern Language Notes,* Vol. 45. pp. 377–387. (June, 1930).

H. T. Baker. "Hazlitt as a Shakespearean Critic." *Publications of the Modern Language Association.* Vol. 47 (1932). pp. 191–199.

P. L. Carver. "Hazlitt's Contributions to the Edinburgh Review," in *Review of English Studies.* IV, 16 ff. (October, 1928).

G. Schnöckelborg. *A. W. Schlegel's Einfluss auf William Hazlitt als Shakespeare-Kritiker.* Emsdetten, 1931.

OTHER WORKS CONSULTED

Addison, Joseph. *See Spectator.*

Alison, Archibald. *Essays on the Nature and Principles of Taste.* Edinburgh, 1790.

Babbitt, Irving. *Rousseau and Romanticism.* Boston and New York, 1919.

Bacon, Francis. *Advancement of Learning,* ed. W. A. Wright. Oxford, 1920.

————. *Novum Organum.* London (Pickering), n. d.

————. *Essays.*

Barry, James. *See* Wornum.

Beers, H. A. *A History of English Romanticism in the Eighteenth Century.* New York, 1899.

————. *A History of English Romanticism in the Nineteenth Century.* New York, 1910.

Blair, Hugh. *Lectures on Rhetoric and Belles Lettres.* London, 1853.

Bosanquet, B. *A History of Æsthetic.* London, 1910.

Bosker, A. *Literary Criticism in the Age of Johnson.* The Hague, 1930.

Burke, Edmund. *An Essay on the Sublime and Beautiful. Works of Edmund Burke,* Vol. I. London, 1881 (Bohn).

Byron, George Gordon Noël, Lord. *Letters and Journals.* ed. Prothero. 6 v. London, 1898–1901.

Campbell, J. D. *See* Coleridge.

Carver, P. L. "The Influence of Maurice Morgann," in *Review of English Studies,* VI (July, 1930). 320–322.

Coleridge, S. T. *See also,* Helmholtz

————. *Samuel Taylor Coleridge; a Narrative of the Events of his Life.* By J. D. Campbell. London, 1894.

————. *Letters of Samuel Taylor Coleridge.* ed. E. H. Coleridge. 2 v. London, 1895.

————. *Unpublished Letters of Samuel Taylor Coleridge.* ed. E. L. Griggs. 2 v. London, 1932.

————. *Coleridge as Philosopher.* By John H. Muirhead. London [1930].

————. *The German Influence on Samuel Taylor Coleridge.* By J. L. Haney. Philadelphia, 1902.

————. *Coleridge on Logic and Learning with selections from the unpublished manuscripts.* By Alice D. Snyder. New Haven, 1929.

————. *Critical Principle of the Reconciliation of Opposites as employed by Coleridge.* By Alice D. Snyder. In *Contributions to Rhetorical Theory.* ed. F. R. Scott. Ann Arbor, 1918.

————. *Anima Poetae.* ed. E. H. Coleridge. Boston, 1895.

————. *Biographia Literaria.* ed. Shawcross. 2 v. Oxford, 1907.

————. *Coleridge's Literary Criticism* with Introduction by J. W. Mackail. London, 1921.

————. *Coleridge's Shakespearean Criticism.* ed. T. M. Raysor. 2 v. Cambridge, 1930.

————. *The Friend.* London, 1885 (Bohn).

————. *Miscellanies, Æsthetic and Literary.* ed. T. Ashe. London, 1885 (Bohn).

———— *Table-Talk and Omniana.* London, 1896 (Bohn).

Daniel, George. *Recollections of Charles Lamb.* London, 1927.

De Quincey, Thomas. *Collected Writings,* ed. D. Masson. 14 v. London, 1896–1897.

Diderot, Denis. *See also* Grimm.

————. *Diderot als Kunstphilosoph.* By Werner Leo. Erlangen, 1918.

————. *Studies in Diderot's Esthetic Naturalism.* By F. Vexler. New York, 1922. (Columbia diss.)

————. *Oeuvres.* 26 v. Paris, 1821–1834. (References in the text are to this edition.)

————. *Oeuvres Complètes.* 20 v. Paris, 1875–1877.

————. *Diderot's Thoughts on Art and Style,* etc. *tr.* B. L. Tollemache. London, 1904.

Dobrée, Bonamy. *Restoration Comedy.* Oxford, 1924.

Dryden, John. *Essays.* ed. W. P. Ker. 2 v. Oxford, 1900.

Farington, Joseph. *The Farington Diary.* ed. J. Greig. 8 v. London, 1922.

Fuseli. *See* Wornum.

Graham, Walter. "Contemporary Critics of Coleridge the Poet." *Publications of the Modern Language Association.* Vol. 38 (1923). pp. 278–289.

Gray, Thomas. *Correspondence of Gray, Walpole, West, and Ashton* . . . ed. P. Toynbee. 2 v. Oxford, 1915.

————. *Works.* ed. Edmund Gosse. New York, 1885. Vols. II and III (*Letters*).

Grimm, Friedrich Melchior, and Diderot, D. *Correspondance Littéraire, Philosophique et Critique.* . . . 16 v. Paris, 1813.

————. *Frederick Melchior Grimm, as a Critic of Eighteenth Century French Drama.* By A. C. Jones. Bryn Mawr, 1926. (Bryn Mawr diss.)

Haney, J. L. *See* Coleridge.

Haydon, B. R. *Autobiography and Memoirs of Benjamin Robert Haydon, 1786–1846.* ed. A. P. D. Penrose. London, 1927.

————. *Correspondence and Table-Talk.* 2 v. London, 1876.

Helmholtz, A. A. *Indebtedness of Samuel Taylor Coleridge to August Wilhelm von Schlegel.* Madison, 1907.

Herrick, M. T. *The Poetics of Aristotle in England.* New Haven, 1930.

Horace. *Horace on the Art of Poetry, Latin.* . . . ed. E. H. Blakeney. London, 1928.

Hume, David. *Essays, Moral, Political, and Literary.* ed. T. H. Green and T. H. Grose. 2 v. London, 1882.

Hunt, Leigh. *Autobiography.* New York, 1850.

————. *Works.* 7 v. London, 1882–91.—*Table Talk,* Vol.

III; *Wit and Humor,* Vol. IV; *Imagination and Fancy,* Vol. V.

————. *Dramatic Essays.* ed. W. Archer and R. W. Lowe. London, 1894.

Johnson, Samuel. *Works.* 13 v. London, 1823.

Jones, A. C. *See* Grimm.

Kames, Lord (Henry Home). *Elements of Criticism.* 7th ed. 2 v. Edinburgh, 1788.

Kant, Emanuel. *See* Willich.

Lamb, Charles. *See also* Daniel.

————. *Life of Charles Lamb.* By E. V. Lucas. 2 v. London, 1905.

————. *Works.* ed. E. V. Lucas. 7 v. London, 1903–1905.

Lessing, G. E. *Selected Prose Works.* tr. E. C. Beasley and H. Zimmern. London, 1879 (Bohn).

Locke, John. *Conduct of the Understanding.* ed. T. Fowler. Oxford, 1901.

Longinus. *Longinus on the Sublime.* tr. A. O. Prickard. Oxford, 1926.

Mengs, Anthony Raphael. *Works.* tr. from Italian. 2 v. London, 1796.

Montaigne, Michel de. *Essays.* tr. Charles Cotton. ed. W. C. Hazlitt. London, 1892.

Morgann, Maurice. *Essay on the Dramatic Character of Sir John Falstaff.* London, 1820.

Moore, Thomas. *Memoirs, Journal, and Correspondence.* ed. Lord John Russell. 8 v. London, 1853–1856.

Morley, John. *Diderot and the Encyclopædists.* 2 v. London, 1891.

Muirhead, John. *See* Coleridge.

Nicoll, Allardyce. *The Theory of Drama.* New York. n. d. [1930?]

Opie. *See* Wornum.

Oxberry, William, ed. *New English Drama.* 22 v. London, 1818–1832.

Paston, G. *Benjamin Robert Haydon and his Friends.* London, 1905.

Pope, Alexander. *Works.* ed. J. W. Croker and W. Elwin. 10 v. London, 1871–1886.

Powell, A. E. *The Romantic Theory of Poetry.* London, 1926.

Raysor, T. M. *See* Coleridge.

Reynolds, Sir Joshua. *Works.* With a memoir by Malone. 3 v. London, 1801.

Richardson, Jonathan. *Works.* London, 1792.

Robinson, H. Crabb. *Blake, Coleridge, Wordsworth, Landor, etc. Being Selections from the Remains of Henry Crabb Robinson.* ed. E. Morley. London, 1922.

————. *The Correspondence of Henry Crabb Robinson with the Wordsworth Circle (1806–66).* ed. E. Morley. Oxford, 1927.

Rousseau, Jean Jacques. *See also* Babbitt.

————. *Confessions.* Complete translation. 2 v. London, 1931 (Everyman).

————. *Eloisa: or, A series of Original Letters.* . . . Translated from the French. London, 1784.

————. *Emile or Education.* tr. B. Foxley. (Everyman).

Saintsbury, George. *A History of Criticism.* 2nd. ed. 3 v. New York, 1905–1908.

Schlegel, A. W. *Lectures on Dramatic Art and Literature.* tr. John Black. London, (1846, Bohn).

————. *Vorlesungen über Dramatische Kunst und Literatur.* ed. G. V. Amoretti. 2 v. Leipsic, 1923.

Shawcross. *See* Coleridge.

Search, Edward (pseud.) *See* Tucker.

Seth, James. *English Philosophers and Schools of Philosophy.* London, 1925.

Smith, Adam. *Theory of Moral Sentiments.* 2 v. London, 1790.

Smith, D. Nichol. *Shakespeare in the Eighteenth Century.* Oxford, 1928.

Snyder, Alice D. *See* Coleridge.

Spectator. 8 v. London, 1827.

Spingarn, J. E. *Critical Essays of the Seventeenth Century.* 2 v. Oxford, 1908.

Steele, Sir Richard. *See Spectator.*

Stephen, Sir Leslie. *History of English Thought in the Eighteenth Century.* 2 v. New York, 1902.

Stewart, Dugald. *Philosophical Essays.* Vol. V of *Collected Works.* Edinburgh, 1854–1860.

Temple, Sir William. *Essays on Ancient and Modern Learning and on Poetry.* Oxford, 1909.

Tucker, Abraham. *The Light of Nature Pursued, by Edward Search, Esq.* 5 v. London, 1768.

Vexler, F. *See* Diderot.

Weber, A. *History of Philosophy,* tr. F. Thilly. New York, 1897.

Whately, Thomas. *Remarks on Some of the Characters of Shakespeare.* Oxford, 1808.

Willich, A. F. M. *Elements of the Critical Philosophy.* . . . London, 1798.

Winckelmann, J. J. *Reflections on the Painting and Sculpture of the Greeks.* . . . tr. H. Fuseli. London, 1765.

Windelband, W. *A History of Philosophy.* tr. J. H. Tufts. New York, 1898.

Wordsworth, William. *Poetical Works.* ed. T. Hutchinson. (with Prefaces, etc.) Oxford, 1916.

————. *Wordsworth's Literary Criticism,* ed. N. C. Smith. London, 1905.

Wornum, R. N., ed. *Lectures on Painting by the Royal Academicians. Barrie, Opie, and Fuseli.* London, 1848 (Bohn).

Young, Edward. *Conjectures on Original Composition,* in Vol. III of *Works.* 3 v. London, 1798.

INDEX